Passport's Illustrated Travel Guide to

HAWAII

FROM
THOMAS
COOK

PASSPORT BOOKS
a division of *NTC Publishing Group*
Lincolnwood, Illinois USA

Published by Passport Books,
an imprint of NTC/Contemporary Publishing
Company,
4255 W. Touhy Avenue,
Lincolnwood (Chicago), Illinois
60646–1975 U.S.A.

Written by Robert Holmes

Original photography by Robert Holmes

Edited, designed, and produced by AA
Publishing.

© The Automobile Association 1996.
Maps © The Automobile Association 1996.

Library of Congress Catalog Card Number: 95-70287

ISBN 0-8442-9001-7

The contents of this publication are believed correct at the time of
printing. Nevertheless the publishers cannot accept responsibility for any
errors or omissions, for changes in the details given in this guide, or for
the consequences of any reliance on the information provided by the
same. Assessments of attractions, hotels, restaurants, and so forth are
based upon the author's own experience and therefore descriptions given
in this guide necessarily contain an element of subjective opinion that
may not reflect the publisher's opinion or dictate a reader's own
experiences on another occasion.
**We have tried to ensure accuracy in this guide, but things do
change and we would be grateful if readers would advise us of any
inaccuracies they may encounter.**

Published by Passport Books in conjunction with AA Publishing and the
Thomas Cook Group Ltd.

Color separation: BTB Colour Reproduction, Whitchurch, Hampshire,
England.

Printed by: Edicoes ASA, Oporto, Portugal.

Second printing 1997.

Contents

About this Book

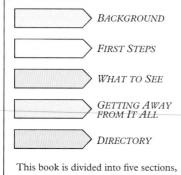

BACKGROUND

FIRST STEPS

WHAT TO SEE

GETTING AWAY
FROM IT ALL

DIRECTORY

This book is divided into five sections, identified by the above color coding.

Dolphins dance the *hula* in an outdoor amphitheatre at Sea Life Park, Hawaii's only marine park, at Makapuu, on Oahu

Background gives an introduction to Hawaii – its history, geography, politics, culture.

First Steps offers practical advice on arriving and getting around.

What to See is an alphabetical listing of places to visit, interspersed with walks and tours.

Getting Away from It All highlights places off the beaten track where it's possible to relax and enjoy peace and quiet.

Directory provides practical information – from shopping and entertainment to children and sports, including a section on business matters. Special highly illustrated features on specific aspects of Hawaii appear throughout the book.

BACKGROUND

The life of the land is
perpetuated in righteousness.
KAMEHAMEHA III
State motto

Introduction

*P*ineapples, palm-fringed beaches backed by rugged green mountains, balmy evenings with gorgeous sunsets, exotic drinks sprouting umbrellas – Hawaii is most people's idea of a dream destination, and for once the dream can come true. With six main islands to choose from, almost anyone can discover their own perfect vacation experience. Whether your interest is in water sports, horseback riding, golf, mountain biking or just lying in the sun on a deserted beach, you can find it there.

It is rare to find such a stress-free tropical environment. Apart from a few nonmalarial mosquitoes, there are no nasty insects in the islands, no snakes, no dangerous animals to worry about, and the Hawaiian people are delightful. A resurgence in ethnic Hawaiian pride has created some racial tension, but this is rarely directed at tourists. The worst thing most visitors have to contend with is bad sunburn.

Culturally, Hawaii is very obviously part of the USA, yet this is tempered by a relaxed Polynesian attitude toward life.

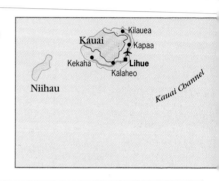

LOCATOR

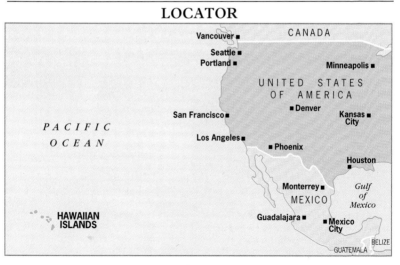

In fact, slowing down to the pace of "island time" can pose initial problems for some visitors. Making the transition easier is the fact that everyone speaks English, travel is easy, and virtually everything you would expect to find on the mainland you will find in Hawaii.

The dream does come at a price, however. Hawaii is thousands of miles from the nearest continent, and

consequently the cost of getting there is high. So, too, is the cost of living. Both hotels and restaurants often charge more than those in major mainland cities. Similarly, prices in supermarkets and shops are higher than on the mainland – occasionally, as in the case of pineapples, inexplicably so.

It's true that there are few real bargains in Hawaii, but given their great beauty the Islands remain very good value for money.

HAWAIIAN ISLANDS

Geography

*H*awaii is the most remote inhabited island group in the world. San Francisco, the closest mainland city, is almost 2,400 miles to the east; Japan and mainland Asia lie over 3,800 miles to the west.

Located in the North Pacific, just south of the Tropic of Cancer, Hawaii forms the northern outpost of Polynesia, whose islands stretch for thousands of miles to the south and west. It also constitutes the southernmost part of the United States, sharing the same latitude as Mexico City, Mecca, Calcutta and Hong Kong.

Although most people think of Hawaii as a small group of islands, there are in fact over 130 in the chain. They stretch in a diagonal arc for an amazing 1,500 miles across the North Pacific, ending in the Kure Atoll and the Midway Islands, which in geological terms are the oldest in the chain. The island of Hawaii – known as the Big Island, to distinguish it from the state name– is currently the

farthest south in the chain. Loihi Seamount, about 30 miles southeast, is getting increasingly close to the ocean surface with successive volcanic eruptions, but with 3,000 feet still to go, it may take more than this writer's lifetime to emerge!

It was a series of massive volcanic eruptions, over 25 million years ago, that began creating a chain of volcanoes (called shield volcanoes) that would become the biggest mountains in the world. The foot of these mountains lies 18,000 feet below the surface of the Pacific Ocean; only their peaks break the surface, to form the Hawaiian Islands. Mauna Kea, the highest point on the Big Island, is 13,796 feet (4,205m) above sea level, making the total height almost 32,000 feet.

The islands were created one at a time from a single group of vents in the Earth's crust, lying close to the junction of two tectonic plates. Hawaii is on the Pacific plate, a portion of the Earth that is moving at a rate of 2 to 3 inches a year. Each time a new mountain formed, it slowly drifted northwest and another mountain would erupt to take its place, until the chain reached its present length of 1,500 miles.

The northernmost islands, which were the first to drift away, are the oldest in the chain; many have been eroded by the sea to become little more than

Falling water thunders into deep pools at Wailuku River State Park in Hilo, Hawaii

Plaits of molten lava pour relentlessly out of Pu'u Halulu, Pu'u 'O'o Vent

desolate atolls and reef banks. In the southeastern end of the chain are the newest islands. Erosion has had little effect on their size, but frequent heavy rains have given them their characteristic knife-edge ridges and deep valleys.

In evolutionary terms, Hawaii is a baby. The newly formed islands were still cooling down when dinosaurs were roaming other parts of the globe. Their geographic isolation added to their evolutionary stagnation. Eventually wind-borne spores brought mosses and ferns to the barren lava fields, birds brought grasses and other seed plants, and insects strayed onto the islands; coral polyps drifted into the shallow waters, and reefs began to form.

Gradually, increasingly diverse life-forms became established and transformed the volcanic desert into the lush islands that we know today.

This is still one of the few places in the world where the whole process of evolution can be observed as it is happening. Active volcanoes continue to create new land mass, new species are still becoming established, and rudimentary coral reef formation continues in the ocean.

Humans are relative newcomers as a species, arriving on the youngest island, Hawaii, probably in the third century A.D. Apart from a military base on Midway Island, only seven of the islands support a permanent population.

History

A.D.300–800

The first Polynesians sail northwest from the Marquesas Islands to the Big Island.

1778

The English Captain James Cook discovers the Sandwich Islands, named for his benefactor, the Earl of Sandwich, and lands on Kauai.

1779

Captain Cook is killed in Kealakekua Bay on the Big Island.

1786

The French explorer Captain La Pérouse lands near Lahaina on Maui.

Captain La Pérouse

1790

The Olowalu Massacre off Maui: over 100 Hawaiians are killed by sea captain Simon Metcalfe.

1791

The English navigator and explorer George Vancouver, after sailing round Lanai, returns to the Big Island and is welcomed by Kamehameha, a leader from a small village who is rapidly becoming the most powerful man in the Islands.

1792

Kamehameha seizes control of the Big Island.

1795

Kamehameha consolidates his control of Maui, grabs Molokai and Lanai, then Oahu.

1796

Kamehameha the Great ascends to the throne.

1810

Kamehameha gains Kauai by peaceful negotiation.

1819

Kamehameha the Great dies, and the kingdom passes to his son, Liholiho, Kamehameha II. The ambitious Kaahumanu, his father's favourite wife, presses him to end the ancient system of *kapu* (taboos) which restricted her powers and put her country at a disadvantage in a rapidly changing world. Kaahumanu declares herself Queen Regent. *Heiaus* (temples) are burned and idols knocked to the ground.

1820

Missionaries arrive from New England.

1823

The first mission is established in Lahaina, Maui.

1824

Liholiho, Kamehameha II, dies.

1825

The kingdom passes to Liholiho's brother Kauikeaouli, Kamehameha III, who is just nine years old.

1835

The first sugar plantation is started on Kauai.

1843
A maverick British naval officer annexes Hawaii to the Crown, but London later countermands his actions.

1850
Foreigners are allowed to purchase land. The Masters and Servants Act starts the flow of Asian immigrants.

1854
Kamehameha III dies after a life of debauchery. The kingdom passes to Alexander Liholiho, Kamehameha IV.

1863
Kamehameha IV dies at age 29, ostensibly from asthma, although drink is thought to be a major factor. His brother Lot succeeds him as Kamehameha V.

1866
The Hawaiian population, ravaged by Western diseases, dwindles to 60,000.

1872
The death of Kamehameha V, who never married, brings the dynasty to an end.

1873
William Lunalilo is elected king by popular vote.

1874
Lunalilo dies and David Kalakaua is elected by a six-to-one majority. "The Merrie Monarch" encourages the preservation of native Hawaiian customs but gives away much of his royal power.

1891
Kalakaua dies and is replaced by his sister, Lydia Liliuokalani, who tries to restore royal powers.

1893
A near bloodless coup deposes Queen Liliuokalani, ending the monarchy.

1898
Hawaii is annexed by the US and given territorial status.

1907
The first US military post, Fort Shafter Army Base, is built.

1919
Pearl Harbor naval base, under construction since 1908, is dedicated.

1922
James Dole buys Lanai and turns the island into the world's largest pineapple plantation.

1936
Pan American inaugurates passenger flights from the mainland.

1941
The Japanese attack Pearl Harbor on the morning of December 7th, bringing America into World War II. Hostility and injustice are directed at Hawaii's many Japanese-Hawaiians.

1959
Hawaii becomes America's 50th state. Tourism greatly increases as the first Boeing 707 jets fly from San Francisco in five hours.

1960
A massive tidal wave strikes Hilo on the Big Island, killing 61 people.

1979
The Office of Hawaiian Affairs is established, highlighting the plight of native Hawaiians.

1982
Hurricane Eva devastates Kauai.

1992
Hurricane Iniki hits Kauai; damage is counted in millions of dollars.

Crest – Royal Mausoleum, Honolulu

EARLY POLYNESIAN

The early Polynesians were probably the greatest sailors the world has known. When Europe was still in the Dark Ages and few ventured beyond the confines of the Mediterranean, whole families of Polynesians were sailing for thousands of miles on uncharted seas in hand-carved canoes with coconut-fibre sails. They first migrated from the coast of Asia about 4,000 years ago, across Indonesia, then island-hopped until finally they arrived in Hawaii, on the Big Island. Navigating by the stars, they could identify over 150 heavenly bodies. The only directions were passed on in legends and chants, while ocean depths and currents were assessed by the color of the water.

It is believed that the Polynesians who arrived in Hawaii were driven from their home islands by war or natural disaster. Groups of families sailed over with their animals, plants and traditions to start a new life on this remote outpost of Polynesia. Their society was based on a caste system: the *ali'i* (chiefs) were at the top, and each chief had a domain that included fishing sites, arable land, and villages. They grew taro and sweet potatoes, hunted wild pigs and caught fish; and there was always an abundance of coconuts

and wild tropical fruits. Each domain had all that was necessary for survival.

Early Hawaiians were a violent and warlike people. They worshipped numerous gods, and to appease them

CULTURE

The ancient craft of basketweaving lives on; above, wooden idols stand on ancient sacred ground at Pu'uhonua o Honaunau, Kona Coast

they practised human sacrifice at their temples (*heiaus*). Often using human bait to fish for sharks, they were also confirmed cannibals. In spite of their almost Stone Age existence with only the most primitive tools, they were able to make fishing nets, clothing and housing all from the coconut palm, and created some of the finest featherwork that has ever been seen.

Until the Islands were "discovered" by the West, there was a harmonious balance between humans and nature.

Population

*M*odern Hawaii is the ultimate cultural melting pot. In 200 years the Islands have been transformed from a totally Polynesian population into the most diverse, integrated society in the US.

When Captain James Cook, sailing for England, arrived in 1778, there were over 300,000 pure Hawaiians in the Islands. By 1876 that number had shrunk to fewer than 60,000. The introduction of gonorrhoea caused sterility, syphilis resulted in stillbirths, and epidemics of cholera, mumps, influenza, measles and smallpox did the rest.

Imported labor

This decimation of the population resulted in a serious shortage in the labor force, and as a countermeasure plantation labor was imported from abroad. In 1852 the Chinese started to arrive; the Japanese in 1868; Portuguese in 1878; Puerto Ricans in 1901; Koreans in 1904; Filipinos in 1907, together with small numbers of immigrants from other countries arriving on an individual basis. Thus the stage was set for the ethnic diversity and cross-cultural society that presently exists.

Today, only one island boasts a totally Hawaiian population – the "Forbidden Island" of Niihau, with just over 200 Hawaiian residents who still speak the native tongue. Non-Hawaiians are not allowed to live on Niihau and, until recently, were not even allowed to visit the island. The population of Molokai is almost 50 percent Hawaiian or predominantly Hawaiian, although that only represents about 2,500 people. On the other islands this figure reaches no more than 20 percent.

For the state as a whole, the figure drops to 12 percent, and many of those 120,000 ethnic Hawaiians have very mixed backgrounds, with only an estimated 1 percent of the population being pure Hawaiian. By contrast, in the middle of the last century 95 percent were pure Hawaiian, with only 1 percent part-Hawaiian.

Rainbow people

The major ethnic groups are Caucasian and Japanese, representing one-third and one-quarter of the population respectively. For most of this century, the Japanese have steadily and consistently emigrated to Hawaii. Caucasians, mostly from the mainland,

Waipio Valley Japanese-American resident

started a gradual migration in the 1920s which accelerated dramatically in the 1960s and 1970s. There continues to be a steady influx of Chinese and Filipinos, who represent 6 and 14 percent of the population respectively. Most African Americans are on military bases.

Although Oahu accounts for less than 10 percent of the state's total land area (590 square miles), this island is home to nearly four out of five of Hawaii's residents. The present density level has been building up for well over a century. In 1831 only a quarter of the population lived on Oahu, and by 1940 it was up to nearly two-thirds.

Half of Oahu's 836,000 people live in Honolulu, the state capital. No other town on the Islands comes close to this massive population. Hilo on the Big Island has fewer than 50,000 people, the biggest town on Maui has under 20,000, and Kapaa on Kauai has under 5,000.

Old or young, Hawaii's ethnic mix is diverse

THE *ALI'I*

In a culture with no written history, the threads of myth and fact can be difficult to disentangle. Descriptions of precontact Hawaii have been handed down through oral tradition.

Hawaii's society was based on a strict caste system, and nobody moved from one caste to another. The *ali'i*, hereditary nobles, were in effect the Hawaiian royalty. They controlled the *makaainana* (commoners), and in between were the *kahuna*, who were a combination of wise man and priest. At the bottom were the *kauwa* (slaves).

Everyone's life was shaped by restrictive laws known as *kapu*, from which our word 'taboo' is derived. Breaking a *kapu* could result in death, even for "offences" like casting a shadow across the house of a chief. Other *kapu*

King Kamehameha the Great. In strengthening links with the West, he paved the way for his descendants (right) to gravitate towards Western tastes in everything from fashion to religion.
Queen Kapiolani (left) enjoyed all Victorian comforts at Iolani Palace

determined the different behavior of the sexes. Men and women were not allowed to eat together, for example, and women could not eat shark, pork, coconuts or bananas. It was laws like these that helped lead to the abolition of *kapu* by Kaahumanu, Kamehameha the Great's favorite wife (out of 21!).

had groups of feather-pluckers whose sole responsibility was to trap birds and collect their countless feathers. One cloak, on display in the Bishop Museum (see page 34), required the yellow upper tail feathers of the predominantly black mamo, now extinct; around 80,000 birds were caught, plucked and released. *Kapa*,

The ancient Hawaiians lived simply, but the *ali'i* wore some of the finest and most spectacular adornments ever made. Cloaks and helmets for the chiefs were made from thousands of intensely colorful feathers. When Captain Cook first saw these, he compared them to the thickest and richest velvet. The chiefs

the finest cloth in Polynesia, was made for the *ali'i* from a type of mulberry bark.

The hereditary caste of *ali'i* flourished, culminating in the great Kamehameha dynasty. But pressures from the outside world continued to grow, and the system finally succumbed in 1893.

Politics

*B*efore World War II Hawaii was controlled by the major economic forces of the day. Sugar was king then, and the Baldwin family of Maui virtually took the place of government. All the most powerful families in the Islands were represented on the boards of the Big Five corporations, which ruled the economy by controlling sugar refining, transportation and utilities.

Above: the Great Seal of Hawaii
Right: the state flag

The only political party during this period was the Republican Party. Queen Liliuokalani's brother, Prince Jonah Kuhio Kalanianaole, formed an alliance with the Republicans, and together they were able to maintain a majority over the large ethnic groups such as the Japanese, Chinese, and Filipinos.

After World War II the Democrats overcame problems with poor leadership and internal fighting. By this time the Japanese were the largest ethnic group in the Islands, and they became politically active. Democrat Jack Burns, a police captain during the war, let it be known that he considered the Japanese-Hawaiians to be exemplary Americans. The Japanese never forgot this and were a major force in getting Burns elected Governor in 1962 and 1966.

The majority of Asian Hawaiians are Democrats, and they have had a significant influence on the political climate. The first member of Congress elected after Hawaii became a state in 1959 was Japanese-American Democrat Daniel Inouye; today he is a senior senator. In 1974 George Ariyoshi became the first ethnic Japanese to be elected governor, and his successor is democrat John Waihee, the first governor of Hawaiian ancestry.

In 1979 the Office of Hawaiian Affairs was created, the first time this century that the rights of native Hawaiians were being addressed. This group has become increasingly vocal, and renewed interest in native Hawaiian heritage, particularly on the part of young people, has even resulted in a strong movement to restore the monarchy.

FIRST STEPS

The Sandwich Islands
remain my idea of the perfect
thing in the matter of
tropical islands.
MARK TWAIN
More Tramps Abroad, 1897

First Steps

ARRIVING

At Honolulu International Airport, only the thick, warm tropical air distinguishes it from any other airport in America. There is no doubt that you have arrived in the Islands – with all that that implies. The airport is clean and efficient, the food outlets are fast and unmemorable.

Although there are direct flights from the mainland to both Maui and the Big Island, most people first fly into Honolulu on Oahu, particularly from international destinations. European visitors can easily tag Hawaii on to a trip to the West Coast. Midweek excursion fares from San Francisco and Los Angeles are usually very competitive. But the best bargains are package deals: for only a little more than the straight airfare, these can include a hotel and even a rental car.

Honolulu is a major Pacific hub, servicing flights between the Far East and the mainland as well as all interisland traffic. There is only one ferry service in operation, that between Molokai and Maui; all other interisland travel has to be by air. If flying on a return ticket from the US mainland or Canada, you can often get good discounts on interisland tickets.

The international and domestic terminals are in separate buildings. A free shuttle, the Wiki Wiki, provides transport between the terminals. Baggage carts are available for $1.50, and the machines accept either the exact change or $1 bills, for which change is given.

GETTING AROUND

The airport is four miles from downtown Honolulu and eight miles from Waikiki. Both can be reached by bus, taxi or limousine. Most visitors, however, rent a car which can be picked up at the airport. Car rental desks are on the ground floor.

Driving is really the only way to get off the beaten track and away from the crowds. Some visitors may be reluctant to drive, especially near Honolulu, where the traffic can appear intimidating, but no one in Hawaii drives very fast. Few drivers exceed the maximum speed limit of 55mph.

PUBLIC TRANSPORT

Outside of Honolulu, public transportation – with the exception of air travel – is not well developed. The public bus service on Oahu is called TheBus, and is rarely used by tourists. It provides the cheapest transportation in the state. Buses operate from 4.30am–1am and provide the best way to come into contact with the people of Hawaii. Information on routes can be found at the Ala Moana Center or by telephoning (808) 848–4444.

Enjoying Nature's air conditioning

Traveling in style: aboard a luxury cruise ship or in a quaint wooden trolley

Taxis are quite expensive. More expensive are pedicabs – bicycle rickshaws.

The Waikiki Trolley is a quaint open-air trolley that travels between Fisherman's Wharf and Kapiolani Park with 29 stops in between. Passengers can get on and off as often as they like. It operates between 9am and 5pm.

There is no passenger rail service.

Kauai's Kokee State Park, set high in the mountains, is ideal for hiking and camping

WHEN TO GO

In general, Hawaii has a very equitable climate. During the day, sea level temperatures rarely fall below 70°F (20°C) and rarely exceed 90°F (30°C) year round. There are no seasons as such, and daytime temperatures in the 80s are usual all year long. The coolest months are February and March and the hottest August and September.

Rain is of greater concern than temperature. Normally the heaviest rains fall between October and April, but it can rain any time. On Mount Waialeale on Kauai, it virtually never stops, with annual precipitation a huge 40 feet!

The weather changes less by season than it does by location. In most cases the major concentration of resort hotels have been built where the sun shines longest and the rain rarely falls. On Oahu this is Waikiki; on Maui, Kaanapali/Kapalua and Wailea; on Kauai, Poipu; and on the Big Island, the South Kohala coast. Prevailing winds determine rainfall, and the windward side of each island tends to be the wettest.

The busiest seasons are from mid-December to Easter and mid-June to early September. At these times prices are higher, especially for hotel rooms, and tourist attractions are crowded.

WHERE TO GO

There is an island to satisfy almost everyone. Three out of every four residents live on Oahu and half of these live in Honolulu, so if it's people and city life you're looking for, this is the place. The North Shore is home of the Banzai Pipeline and world-class surfing. Kauai is the prettiest and most lush, with idyllic beaches and stunning mountains. The hiking and sea-kayaking on Kauai are among the world's best.

Lanai has only 20 miles of paved road and a population of 2,000. It's not the most picturesque island, but its two exclusive resorts offer a unique escape. Molokai is not developed for tourism and is perhaps the closest you can get to the feeling of old Hawaii. The island has beautiful deserted beaches and dramatic mountains, but nothing in the way of nightlife or entertainment. Maui is just the opposite. West Maui is a throbbing center of activity, with huge resorts very popular with younger visitors. The Wailea coast is much more sedate and upscale. Haleakala and the Hana Coast provide some of the best unspoilt countryside in Hawaii.

Hawaii, the Big Island, has a series of exclusive resorts on the sun-drenched Kohala Coast, 13,000-foot-high volcanoes and the biggest privately owned ranch in America. The Kona Coast is the center for big-game fishing.

LIFESTYLE

Hawaii has the same lifestyle and conventions of etiquette as the mainland – and most of the Western world, for that matter – but perhaps because it is always summertime in Hawaii, the living is easier. Formality for men means wearing pants instead of shorts; for women almost any dress or pants are acceptable.

Even in the formal restaurants of the best hotels, men are rarely required to wear jackets or ties. Casual elegance is the usual dress requirement in the islands, and the range of opinion as to what constitutes elegance appears to be very broad.

Aloha is the universal Hawaiian word of greeting and love, and the *aloha* spirit of welcome has become a slogan for the Islands. Fridays have been designated Aloha Friday, when even the most formal businesspeople and conservative civil servants shed their suits in favour of floral *aloha* prints. This tolerant casualness extends to punctuality, hence the popular euphemism for being late: "Hawaiian time."

Bright colors are the order of the day

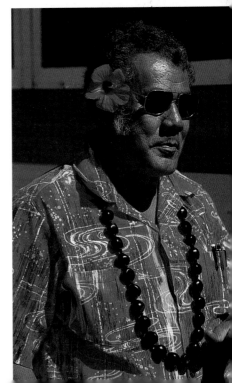

LANGUAGE

English is the universal language of the Islands. Virtually everyone speaks it, although in some areas popular with Japanese visitors, particularly shops, English is becoming very much less predominant. Of course, the original language of the Islands is Hawaiian, closely related to other Polynesian tongues. In spite of the almost total use of English as the primary language, several Hawaiian words have slipped into everyday usage. For example, listening to traffic and weather reports on the radio you'll hear the words *mauka* and *makai* cropping up in every sentence. To any islander the meaning is as obvious as saying left and right, only with much more relevance to island life. *Mauka* means towards the mountains and *makai* means towards the sea.

The pure Hawaiian words in common use are soon learned, even by a visitor, but just when you think you have them mastered, you hear another language that makes no sense at all. "Pidgin" was developed during the plantation era as a means of communication between the diverse ethnic groups working in the fields. The basis is English combined with Hawaiian, but with a smattering of Chinese, Samoan, Japanese and Tagalog (principal language of the Philippines). It is learned in school playgrounds and is commonly used on the streets; the problem with learning it is that it changes from generation to generation. "Pidgin" is constantly evolving, and only those who live with it can really understand its subtleties.

At one time there was an academic movement to exterminate "pidgin," but most islanders feel it contributes to local style and should be preserved. Pidgin is now officially sanctioned by the State.

Basic Hawaiian

To the uninitiated, Hawaiian looks like a random scattering of vowels with the odd **m**, **k** and **h** thrown in, in no particular order. Take the state fish, for example, the *humuhumunukunukuapuaa*. Just pronounce every letter and you've mastered the language – well, nearly!

There are only 12 letters in the alphabet, all the vowels plus **h**, **k**, **l**, **m**, **n**, **p** and **w**. The **a** is pronounced as in *ah*, the **e** as in gr*e*y, the **i** as in f*ee*t, the **o** as in p*o*ny, and the **u** as in b*oo*t.

a'a	a type of rough volcanic lava. Geologists have universally adopted the word to describe this type of lava
ae	yes
ali'i	a Hawaiian chief
aloha	the common form of greeting and farewell
aole	no
hale	house
haole	white person; originally it meant foreigner
hapa	half
hapa haole	half-Caucasian
heiau	a Hawaiian temple with wooden buildings on a platform of fitted rocks; usually only the rocks remain
hula	a Hawaiian dance
huli huli	barbecue
imu	an underground oven where the food is cooked by hot rocks
kahuna	a priest; in old Hawaii they were more like witch doctors, with the power to heal or destroy

kalua	roasted underground in an *imu*, as in *kalua* pig	*tapa*	a traditional cloth made from tree bark
kamaaina	an island resident of any ethnic background. *Kamaaina* rates are offered on everything from plane fares to meals	*tutu*	a grandmother
		ukulele	a small stringed instrument – one of the few Hawaiian words to achieve international meaning
kane	man; commonly used for men's room	*wahine*	young woman. Commonly used for women's room
kapu	keep out, forbidden	*wiki*	fast
kapuna	a wise elder	*wiki wiki*	very fast
keiki	child or children. Many hotels have *keiki* programs		
lanai	veranda or balcony		
lei	a garland, traditionally of flowers or vines		
lomilomi	traditional Hawaiian massage		
luau	a Hawaiian feast		
mahalo	thank you		
makai	towards the sea		
mauka	towards the mountains		
mauna	mountain		
moana	the ocean		
muumuu	voluminous dress for women, introduced by missionaries		
ohana	family, in the broadest sense		
ono	tastes good		
pa'hoehoe	smooth volcanic lava. Geologists have universally adopted the word to describe this type of lava		
pali	cliff		
paniolo	Hawaiian cowboy		
poi	pounded taro (very much an acquired taste!)		
puka	a hole		
pu pu	an appetizer. Receptions often offer heavy *pu pus*, which can easily substitute for dinner		

The Best of Hawaii

ADVENTURE

Big Island: helicopter flight over Kilauea. **Kauai:** kayaking the Na Pali Coast (see page 72). **Lanai:** jeep ride to the Garden of the Gods (see page 133). **Maui:** seeing the Hana Coast on horseback. **Molokai:** hiking down to Kalaupapa (see page 130). **Oahu:** kayaking to Molukua off Lanikai Beach.

BEACHES

Big Island: Hapuna Beach. **Kauai:** Secret Beach (see page 138). **Lanai:** Polihua Beach. **Maui:** Oneloa Beach. **Molokai:** Moomomi Beach. **Oahu:** Mokuleia Beach (see pages 138–9).

CRUISES

Big Island: The Discovery, Kailua-Kona. **Oahu:** American Hawaii Cruises; Windjammer Cruises (both Honolulu).

HOTELS

Big Island: Mauna Lani Bungalows (see page 121). **Kauai:** Hyatt Regency. **Lanai:** Lodge at Koele. **Maui:** Hana-Maui (see page 85). **Oahu:** Halekalani.

DIVING

Big Island: Napoopoo Beach Park. **Kauai:** snorkelling off Niihau. **Lanai:** The Cathedrals in Hulopoe Bay. **Maui:** Molokini Island. **Oahu:** Hanauma Bay.

FOOD

Big Island: the *luau* at Kona Village. **Kauai:** dinner at a Pacific Café. **Lanai:** any meal at The Lodge at Koele. **Maui:** lunch at Hailemaile General Store. **Molokai:** breakfast at Kualapuu Cook House. **Oahu:** a refreshing shave ice at S Matsumoto's (see page 57).

HIKING

Big Island: Volcanoes National Park (see pages 102 and 118). **Kauai:** Kalalau Trail (see page 68). **Lanai:** Garden of the Gods (see page 133). **Maui:** into the Haleakala crater (see page 84). **Molokai:** Halawa Valley to Hipuapua Falls (see pages 128–9). **Oahu:** Diamond Head (see page 40).

HISTORIC SITES

Big Island: Pu'uhonua o Honaunau National Historic Park (see page 112). **Kauai:** Menehune Ditch (see page 72). **Lanai:** Luahiwa petroglyphs (see page 134). **Maui:** Bailey House Museum (see page 80). **Molokai:** Iliiliopae Heiau (see page 130). **Oahu:** *Arizona* Memorial (see pages 32–3).

SURFING

Big Island: Hunnels, south of Kailua. **Kauai:** Anini Beach. **Maui:** Hookipa Beach. **Oahu:** Waimea Beach.

VIEWS

Big Island: Waipio Valley from the Lookout (see pages 117 and 142). **Kauai:** Kalalau Lookout (see page 68). **Lanai:** looking from Munro Trail across to Molokai (see page 134). **Maui:** rim of Haleakala crater at dawn (see page 84). **Molokai:** Kalaupapa Lookout (see page 131). **Oahu:** Mount Tantalus (see page 47).

WATERFALLS

Big Island: Akaka Falls (see page 98). **Kauai:** Wailua Falls (see page 75). **Maui:** Oheo Gulch (see page 90). **Molokai:** Halawa Valley Falls (see pages 128–9). **Oahu:** Sacred Falls.

WHAT TO SEE

Somebody said to me,
when I told them I was going
round the world, that I would
find Honolulu "up to sample."
It most certainly is
**ALFRED VISCOUNT
NORTHCLIFFE,**
1923

Oahu

*V*irtually every visitor to Hawaii comes to Oahu. All major international flights stop at Honolulu Airport, and many visitors never get beyond the Waikiki crowds a few miles away. Both tourism and defense support the economy of Oahu. Ironic, then, that this is the major island destination for Japanese tourists, for it was the Japanese attack here at Pearl Harbor that brought America into World War II in 1941.

Oahu, with 6 million visitors a year, is often dismissed as an overcrowded tourist trap. Certainly there are crowds if you want them, but drive for an hour and the island is as rural and unspoilt as any in

the chain. Although small, it is packed with features and attractions to keep even the most jaded traveler entertained.

Oahu is the second oldest island in the Hawaiian chain. Long ago it was two separate islands, which were joined 2 million years ago when the Leilehua Plateau emerged from the sea. Two dramatic mountain ranges rise up on either side, the Waianae Range and the Koolau Range, both of which create an impressive backdrop to the coast and the plantations inland.

Pineapple plantations are still the major feature of central Oahu. They coexist with sugarcane fields and extensive military barracks.

The North Shore has virtually no major development. The small settlements are either old sugar mill towns or a mixture of craft shops, art galleries and the odd café strung out along the main road. Every winter this coast takes a beating from some of the fiercest surf in the world, and the Banzai Pipeline presents the ultimate challenge to surfers.

The Windward Coast is the most dramatic on the island. The curving Kamehameha Highway follows this rugged coastline backed by the sheer walls of the Koolau Range.

Chinaman's Hat Island, a name that recalls Hawaii's earliest imported labor group

Rows of baby pineapples, surviving in a world of stiff international competition

OAHU

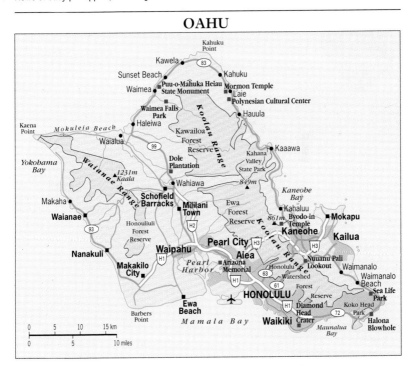

Kahuku Point
Kawela
Kahuku
Sunset Beach
Puu-o-Mahuka Heiau   Mormon Temple
Waimea   State Monument   Laie
Polynesian Cultural Center
Waimea Falls
Park   Hauula
Kaena   Mokuleia Beach   Haleiwa
Point   Kawailoa
Waialua   Forest
Reserve   Kahana
Valley/   Kaaawa
State Park
Yokohama   Dole
Bay   Plantation
1231m   Wahiawa   849m
Kaala
Kaneohe
Bay
Schofield   Ewa
Makaha   Barracks   Mililani   Kahaluu
Town   Forest   861m   Byodo-in   Mokapu
Waianae   Reserve   Temple
Honouliuli   Kaneohe   Kailua
Forest   H2
93   Reserve   Pearl City   H3
Waipahu   Aiea   H3
Nanakuli   H1   Nuuanu Pali
Pearl   Arizona   Lookout   Waimanalo
Makakilo   Harbor   Memorial   Honolulu   Waimanalo
City   61   Watershed   Beach
H1   Forest   Sea Life
HONOLULU   Reserve   Park
Ewa   Diamond   Koko Head
Barbers   Beach   H1   Head   Park   Halona
Point   Waikiki   Crater   72   Blowhole
Mamala Bay   Maunalua
Bay

Koolau Range
Waianae Range
Koolau Range

0   5   10   15 km
0   5   10 miles

HONOLULU

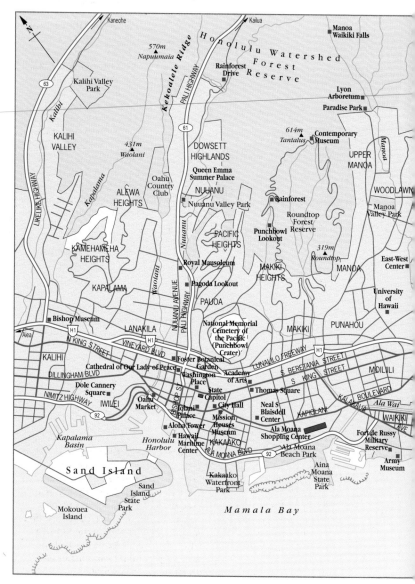

Honolulu

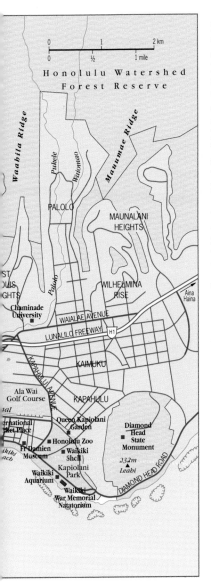

Honolulu is dominated by the extinct volcanic cone Diamond Head, at the far end of Waikiki. It is a big city, the 10th largest in the US. There are really two main parts to Honolulu as far as the tourist is concerned. The downtown district is the business and financial center of the whole Pacific region and has many of the island's most historic buildings rubbing shoulders with high-rise business towers (see pages 60–1). The only royal palace in America is located here, along with Chinatown.

To most visitors, though, the heart of the city is Waikiki. This narrow strip of sand, lined almost exclusively with hotels, restaurants and shops, has become one of the world's most famous beaches. Its popularity with tourists from Japan is such that a whole Japanese culture has developed, and the English language has become almost a novelty.

Inevitably Honolulu has all the problems associated with large urban populations. Traffic is impossible. The system of one-way streets is extremely frustrating, and unfamiliar Hawaiian street names exacerbate the situation. But even without these irritations, there are just too many cars on the road and too few parking spaces.

Crime, unfortunately, is also a reality. Valuables should never be left in parked cars, either in the city or anywhere else on the island. Rental cars are a target all too easily identified. Prostitution is a problem in Waikiki, but it is usually Japanese men who are targeted. Having said all this, Honolulu is not as bad as cities of a similar size throughout the world. Apart from theft, tourists have very little to worry about.

ALOHA TOWER

When it was built in 1926 as the harbor control tower, this was the tallest building in Hawaii (see page 60). The 184-foot, 10-story building is now dwarfed by the high-rises of downtown Honolulu, but its significance remains as great as ever. In the days of steamer travel, this was the first and last landmark seen by the passengers. The "Aloha" greeting prominently displayed atop the four sides of the tower came to symbolize Hawaii. A lift gives access to the 10th-floor observation deck, which gives sweeping views of the harbor and an interesting perspective of the downtown office buildings reflecting both the city and the harbor. On the ninth floor is a small museum of Honolulu Harbor history. The tower and surrounding buildings have recently been undergoing extensive renovation, which was completed in 1995. The new complex includes shops and restaurants.
Pier 9. Tel: (808) 529–4400. Open: daily, 8am–9pm Free.

ARIZONA MEMORIAL

Pearl Harbor will always have a chilling significance for Americans. Because of events that took place here on December 7, 1941, the United States entered World War II. Just before 8 o'clock on a beautiful morning, Japanese fighters attacked, killing or wounding 3,581 Americans, sinking six ships and damaging or destroying 347 planes. One ship, the USS *Arizona*, sank with 1,102 men on board, whose remains are still entombed there. This macabre site is the number-two tourist attraction in all Hawaii, and most Americans, from whatever generation, find that the memorial evokes great emotion. It is nevertheless a sobering experience to visit this national shrine.

Visits start at the Arizona Memorial Visitor Center, run jointly by the National Park Service and the navy. The exhibit is a pictorial history with a strong emphasis on the involvement of the Japanese-Hawaiians during the war. Models show the *Arizona* as it was in 1941 and as it is today. And a film reviews the basic facts of the atttack. The gift shop and bookstore specialise in World War II and Hawaiiana.

Greetings from Honolulu: the Aloha Tower rises by the water's edge at Pier 9

A marble shrine is carved with the name of every sailor who died aboard the *Arizona* back in 1941

The Memorial itself is a long, graceful alabaster structure set above the USS *Arizona*, which still lies on the bottom of Pearl Harbor, its shadowy hull clearly visible through the water. A launch takes people from the Visitor Center to the Memorial, and the complete tour takes about 75 minutes. Tickets are issued on a first-come, first-served basis; to avoid long waits, visit early in the morning. Appropriate dress is required (no bare feet or swimsuits allowed). Children under 45 inches tall are not admitted.

Private operators also run harbor tours out of Kewalo Basin, but passengers are not allowed to disembark at the Memorial.

1 Arizona Memorial Place. Tel: (808) 422–0561. Open: daily 8am–3pm (Memorial); 7:30am–5pm (Visitor Center and Museum). Admission charge. By car: take H–1 West to exit 15A and follow the signs. By bus: take no 50, 51 or 52 from Ala Moana Center or no 20 from Waikiki; all stop by the Memorial entrance. Shuttle bus from major Waikiki hotels (small fee). Tel: (808) 926–4747.

PEARL HARBOR

As early as the 1870s Pearl Harbor was being eyed by the US as a strategic port, but opposition to leasing Hawaiian land put a stop to these ideas. In 1887 America was finally granted an exclusive right to use Pearl Harbor as a port. The harbor was historically used for oyster-growing, and until early this century it was a shallow lagoon. Extensive dredging made the harbor navigable – and a fateful home for the US Navy's Pacific fleet.

The Army Museum, Battery Randolph, by one of the least crowded of Waikiki's beaches

BATTERY RANDOLPH

The Fort De Russy Army Museum occupies the long bunker-like Battery Randolph at the end of Waikiki Beach. Walls 22 feet thick made the building almost impossible to demolish without badly damaging surrounding buildings, so it was given a new life as a very professionally presented museum. A display of tanks greets you outside, while inside is exhibited every type of weapon used in modern warfare, along with a few less modern instruments, such as Hawaiian war clubs embedded with shark's teeth. Other exhibits illustrate the manufacture of ammunition and bombs. *Kalia and Saratoga Roads. Tel: (808) 438–2821. Open: Tuesday to Sunday 10am–4.30pm. Free.*

BISHOP MUSEUM

This is the State Museum of Natural and Cultural History and is a major scientific institution, housing the world's finest collections relating to both Hawaii and the whole Pacific region. The 12-acre site also accommodates a large collection of plants, a library, museum archives, a museum shop and a cafeteria. Come on a weekend to avoid large groups of children on field trips.

The museum was founded by Charles Reed Bishop in 1889 as a memorial to his wife, Princess Bernice Pauahi, the last direct descendant of King Kamehameha. Her family heirlooms formed the basis for the museum's collection. But the Bishop Museum is now much more than a setting for Hawaiiana. In addition to

Hawaiian and Pacific artifacts, there are birds and mammals, fish specimens, land and sea shells, and millions of insect specimens – the largest collection of Pacific natural history in the world.

The Planetarium has daily shows using state-of-the-art audio and video. The adjoining Observatory is open on Fridays and Saturdays, weather permitting. The Cooke Rotunda has exhibits of animated maps and push-button displays.

The hands-on Hall of Discovery, with a children's center, has Hawaiian toys, pre-contact tools, large turtle shells to crawl under, and petroglyph images to color. Changing exhibits often feature photography or painting.

Another building houses Atherton Halau, where the *hula* dance is performed daily, except Sunday. Demonstrations of Hawaiian crafts include *lei*-making, featherwork and basket-weaving.

The three floors of the Hawaiian Hall are a fine example of a classic Victorian museum display, with a central area that stages lunchtime recitals of Hawaiian music and dance performances. The exhibits are outstanding items that once belonged to the Hawaiian monarchy, together with artifacts from the early explorers of Polynesia. Hanging from the ceiling is a 50-foot-long sperm whale.

The cultural displays of the adjoining Polynesian Hall cover the whole Pacific region. Next door is the Kahili Room, with changing exhibits. The Hall of Hawaiian Natural History describes the volcanic formation of the land and development of Hawaii's unique life-forms. The Vestibule Gallery displays folk arts and crafts.

1525 Bernice Street (junction of H–1 freeway and Likelike Highway). Tel: (808) 847–3511. Open: daily 9am–5pm. Observatory: Friday and Saturday 7.30am–9pm, weather permitting. Closed: Christmas. Admission charge.
Planetarium shows at 11am and 2pm, also at 7pm Friday and Saturday.
Atherton Halau: hula performances 1pm Monday to Saturday.

Left: one of the many outstanding exhibits at the world-class Bishop Museum (below)

LEIS

The beautiful, fragrant flower garlands called *leis* are as much a symbol of the Hawaiian Islands as *hula* dancers. At one time it was impossible to imagine visiting the Islands without receiving at least one *lei* greeting.

No one knows the origin of these colorful garlands. The favoured *lei* of old Hawaii was made from the scented green leaves of the *maile* vine; old-timers still consider this to be the finest *lei* of all.

Each island has its own special and uniquely colored version of the *lei*. For the Big Island it is made from the scarlet *lehua* flower. Maui has adopted a pink rose known as *lokelani*, meaning "rose of heaven." It should really be *roselani*, but as neither the "r" nor the "s" occurs in the Hawaiian alphabet, it is pronounced *lokelani*.

Oahu has a *lei* made from the tiny yellow *ilima* flower; it is rarely seen because of the difficulty in collecting the hundreds of flowers needed for a single garland. It used to be restricted to the decoration of chieftains and royalty. The *lei* for Kauai is made from a small purple fruit called a *mokihana*, which is native to the island. On Molokai the

lei is made from the flowers and silver-green leaves of the *kukui* tree. The orange *lei* of Lanai is made from the strange parasitic plant called dodder in English and *kaunaoa* in Hawaiian.

On the tiny island of Niihau the *lei* is not made from plants at all but from the exquisite, tiny Niihau shells that are found on the beaches of this "Forbidden Island." The finest Niihau *leis* are worth

Skillful fingers and the abundance of Nature are required to produce the glorious garlands that symbolize Hawaii. Opposite, from top: Niihau's shell *leis*; a rainbow of choice; *lei*-making at the Sheraton Moana Surfrider Hotel, Waikiki. This page: sun-toned *leis* at the Old Lahaina Luau, Maui; *leis* at Waikiki

a considerable amount of money.

The *leis* usually given to visitors are made from fragrant *plumeria* blooms. They are often presented at fine hotels and *luaus* throughout the Islands, although shell *leis* are becoming more common for reasons of cost.

Many hotels give *lei*-making demonstrations, as does the Bishop Museum in Honolulu.

and herb shops. The best way to experience it is on foot (see pages 58–9). Two of the groups that offer tours are: *Chinatown Historic Society, 1250 Maunakea Street. Tel: (808) 521–3045. Open: Monday to Saturday 10am and 1pm. Admission charge. Hawaii Heritage Center, 1128 Smith Street. Tel: (808) 521–2749. Open: Friday 9:30am and 12:30pm. Admission charge.*

Chinatown's restaurants and shops cater for the hungry, or simply curious, visitor

CHINATOWN

The Chinese first came to Hawaii as contract laborers in the mid-1800s to work on the sugar-cane plantations. Within 10 years they owned the majority of stores in Honolulu – and thus was born Honolulu's first Chinatown. In 1886 the area suffered a serious fire; then in 1900 another fire, started to control bubonic plague, got out of control and destroyed the whole area. A new Chinatown emerged from the ashes, lining the streets with the two-story wooden buildings that can be seen today. It is an authentic Asian community with all the attendant noodle shops, temples

CONTEMPORARY MUSEUM

This remarkable museum, showing the finest contemporary art in all media, is as notable for its setting as its collection. Located in the Makiki Heights on Mount Tantalus, it has panoramic views of Honolulu from large landscaped gardens with descending lawns, a secluded ravine in which to meditate, and sculptures. Five galleries in the main building have changing exhibits by both local and international artists. The Milton Cades Pavilion has a walk-in environment by David Hockney, inspired by Ravel's opera *L'Enfant et les Sortileges*. The permanent collection also includes works by Jim Dine, Josef Albers, Frank Sella, Robert Arneson and photographer William Wegman. The Contemporary

APOSTLE OF THE LEPERS

In 1864 a new law decreed that all lepers must be banished to Molokai, to fend for themselves. That same year, a handsome young Belgian arrived in Hawaii as a missionary. When Father Damien was allowed to go to Molokai in 1873, he found nearly 800 lepers living in squalor and stench, the dying being tended by those less diseased. Card games, quarrels and alcohol were their main pursuits. Father Damien, strong in body and sweet in temperament, dressed their sores, fed them, even made their coffins. He cared for their souls and also their material needs, building homes, teaching the children, arranging for regular supplies of food, encouraging the stronger men to grow crops. His example drew a few others, including a doctor, to serve on Molokai. Over a period of time, the lepers' despair was replaced by new hope and courage. After 11 years Father Damien contracted leprosy, as he always knew he would, but continued his work as "the happiest missioner in the world" until his death five years later, at age 49.

Café serves superb lunches.

The museum has a more accessible branch at the Alana Waikiki Hotel, featuring Hawaii's best artists.
Contemporary Museum, 2411 Makiki Heights Drive. Tel: (808) 526–1322. Open: Tuesday to Saturday 10am–4pm, Sunday noon–4pm. Closed: major holidays. Café – open: daily 11am–3:30pm, Sunday 11am–2pm. Admission charge.
Alana Waikiki Hotel, 1956 Ala Moana Boulevard. Tel: (808) 941–7275.

DAMIEN MUSEUM

This small museum is dedicated to Father Damien, one of the great missionaries of all time. The photographs and artifacts, however, hardly do justice to a man who gave his life for Hawaiian lepers. (See Kalaupapa on page 130.)
130 Ohua Avenue, behind St Augustine's Church. Tel: (808) 923–2690. Open: Monday to Friday 9am–3pm, Saturday 9am–noon. Admission and parking are free.

Three-dimensional poolside art: a witty yet provocative statement, Contemporary Museum

Long dead yet still majestic, the volcano of Diamond Head looms over manmade constructions

DIAMOND HEAD

Many visitors don't realize that Diamond Head is more than just the most prominent landmark in Honolulu. A road curving round from Kapiolani Park passes through a tunnel directly into the crater of this extinct volcano. There is a military base here, but also one of the most memorable walks on the island. It winds for three-quarters of a mile to the very top of Diamond Head, affording grand views over Waikiki. The whole experience can be completed within 90 minutes, and is great fun with a particularly rewarding finish.

Take Kalakaua Avenue until it meets Diamond Head Road and follow this into the crater. From the parking lot at the road head, take a level concrete path that leads towards the summit. The

going looks deceptively easy, but within 200 yards the level concrete changes to a steep, rocky trail. After 15 minutes, 60 steps lead to a sign stating that flashlights (torches) are needed on the trail, followed by a long, very dark tunnel. Of course, few people arrive at this point with a flashlight, but after getting this far, not many turn back! The tunnel experience becomes a group project as people traveling in both directions struggle to find their way. Just when daylight appears ahead and you think it's all over, you turn a corner and there are 100 steps leading straight up. The top of the stairs must, you hope, be the summit – but no. Awaiting you is another totally dark, circular staircase housed in an old bunker. Once this is successfully negotiated, you crawl through one of the

bunker slits – to see the whole of Waikiki spread out before you.
Diamond Head State Monument. Tel: (808) 587–0285. Open: daily 6am–6pm. Free.

DOLE CANNERY SQUARE

Pineapples used to be big business, and the Dole Company was a major player. At its zenith 2 million pineapples a day were processed here. Until recently their cannery still operated in Honolulu, and one of the main reasons to visit the Square was to see it in operation. Now, however, the closest you can come to encountering pineapples is watching *The Pineapple Story*, shown every 20 minutes in the Square's cinema. Apart from that, there are shops and more shops and an uninspiring fast-food outlet. A free shuttle bus to the Square leaves Waikiki every 20 minutes between 8am and 4pm.
650 Iwilei Road. Tel: (808) 548–6600/ 6601. Open: daily 9am–5pm. Free.

EAST-WEST CENTER

The University of Hawaii campus in the Manoa Valley is unremarkable except for the 21 acres that comprise the East-West Center. It was dedicated by Congress in 1960 to promote better relations with the countries of Asia and the Pacific. Most of the buildings display works of art, but several of the buildings are noteworthy themselves, including architect I. M. Pei's Imin Conference Center. Hawaiian and Korean architects designed the Center for Korean Studies, inspired by Kyongbok Palace in Seoul. The Thai Pavilion, a gift from the King of Thailand, was built there, then reconstructed in Hawaii. (Self-guided tour maps from the lobby of John A Burns Hall, plus information on events.)
1777 East-West Road. Tel: (808) 944–7111. Open: Monday to Friday 8am–4:30pm. Free.

Atop a lookout point on Diamond Head

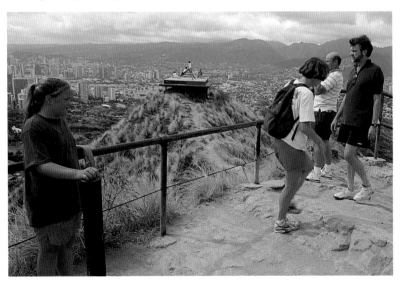

FOSTER BOTANICAL GARDEN

Right in the heart of downtown
Honolulu are 20 acres of wonderful
tranquillity. Back in the 1850s Dr
Hillebrand planted some of the
magnificent trees that now make this the
flagship site of the Honolulu Botanical
Garden. Never overcrowded, these
mature gardens are an extremely pleasant
escape from the surrounding urban area.
Self-guided tour booklets are available
free at the visitor's center.
*50 North Vineyard Boulevard. Tel: (808)
522-7066. Open: daily 9am–4pm. Closed:
Christmas and New Year's. Admission
charge.*

GRAVE AFFAIRS
(Royal Mausoleum)

A tropical island vacation resort may seem
an unlikely place for graveyard tours, but
in addition to the National Memorial
Cemetery of the Pacific, in the extinct
crater called Punchbowl (see page 48),
there are some other sites worthy of note.

Alexander Cartwright, the inventor of
baseball who died in 1892, is buried in a
pink granite tomb in Oahu Cemetery.
Close by is the Royal Mausoleum, the
most important burial place in the
Islands. Buried here are kings
Kamehameha II through King
Kamehameha V, King Kalakaua and
Queen Liliuokalani. The chapel was
designed by Hawaii's first architect,
Theodore Heuck.

Monarch's final resting place, Royal Mausoleum

King Lunalilo felt scorned by
members of the Kamehameha dynasty
and refused to be buried with them. He
requested a private tomb on the grounds
of Kawaiaha'o Church (see page 46) so
that he could be closer to his people.
King Kamehameha IV married Queen
Emma in the church, and later King
Lunalilo took his oath of office there.
*Kawaiaha'o Church, Punchbowl Street at
South King Street.*

The *Falls of Clyde*, nowadays a museum, once
carried oil and sugar across the Pacific

A cool, blue pool is the focal point of this courtyard at the Academy of Arts

Oahu Cemetery, 2162 Nuuanu Avenue.
Royal Mausoleum, 2261 Nuuanu Avenue.
Tel: (808) 536–7602. Open: Monday to
Friday 8am–4:30pm. Free.

HAWAII MARITIME CENTER

The world's last four-masted, full-rigged
sailing ship, the *Falls of Clyde* (see page
60), floats at its mooring beside the
Maritime Center, next to the Aloha
Tower. The Scottish-built ship used to
sail into Honolulu *en route* from San
Francisco over a century ago, when the
harbor would have been packed with
similar vessels. Now the last remaining
ship of its kind has become a museum.
It's an appropriate adjunct to the Hawaii
Maritime Center, one of the finest
museums devoted to seafaring in
existence. Two floors of well-conceived
exhibits trace the sea's role in the history
of Hawaii, from the early Polynesians to
Captain Cook and the steamship
companies. An outstanding audio tour
that leads visitors through the exhibits is
included in the admission.
Pier 7, Honolulu Harbor. Tel: (808)
536–6373. Open: daily 9am–5pm.
Admission charge. Free parking is available
next to the Center, but the location is not

obvious; ask for directions at the Center's
entrance.

HONOLULU ACADEMY OF ARTS

The Academy of Arts is the only general
art museum in the state of Hawaii. In
1927 the Mediterranean-influenced
building opened to the public with an
already established collection of
Japanese and Chinese art. This has
since been expanded to become one of
the finest Asian art collections in the
world. Author James Michener decided
to donate his outstanding collection of
Japanese *ukiyoe* prints to the Academy
rather than to a New York museum.
Although the Asian collection is still the
most important, an impressive
collection of Western art has also been
amassed, including works by Gauguin,
Cézanne and Monet. The Academy's
28 galleries surround six garden
courtyards, providing one of the most
delightful art gallery environments
imaginable.
900 South Beretania Street. Tel: (808)
532–8701. Open: Tuesday to Saturday
10am–4:30pm (guided tour 11am),
Sunday 1–5pm (guided tour 1pm).
Donation appreciated.

The Renaissance-style Iolani Palace served briefly as a prison for Queen Liliuokalani

African wildlife. This state-of-the-art exhibit is now home to over 40 mammals, birds and reptiles, from lions and rhinoceros to sacred ibis and secretary birds. One of the most impressive attractions is the world's first breeding colony of the giant Galapagos tortoise.

Elephant Encounter is presented daily at 11am, and occasionally at 1:30pm, in the Elephant Pavilion. Children love to watch the elephants go through their performance in what amounts to an educational circus. The Children's Zoo is the usual friendly, tactile encounter with domesticated animals. Every Wednesday evening from June to August "The Wildest Show in Town" is free, featuring different entertainment each week. The attractions are listed in newspapers and on posters around Waikiki. Gates reopen at 5pm for this event.

151 Kapahulu Avenue. Tel: (808) 971–7171. Open: daily 9am–4:30pm. Closed: Christmas and New Year's. Admission charge.

HONOLULU *HALE*

Honolulu City Hall is, like so many Honolulu buildings, a curious mixture of styles. The main building is California Spanish-style dating from 1929; the central courtyard is modeled on the 13th-century Bargello Palace in Florence, Italy, and the materials are coral and crushed Hawaiian sandstone. Exhibits are shown in the courtyard.

530 South King Street. Tel: (808) 523–4385. Open: Monday to Friday 8am–4:30pm. Closed: all holidays. Free.

HONOLULU ZOO

The zoo occupies 42 acres of Kapiolani Park below Diamond Head. Recent renovations and new exhibits have brought the zoo up to international standard. There are 350 species on display, of which 42 are endangered. A recently completed 10-acre African savanna exhibit replicates the habitat of

HOTEL STREET

The most notorious street in Honolulu cuts right through Chinatown. Hotel Street has always been the city's red-light area, and during the 1800s it was a popular destination for sailors whose ships were docked a few blocks away, where the Aloha Tower now stands. Over 300 prostitutes worked on the street in those days. Today it is a seedy collection of "adult" cinemas, topless bars and porn shops. The ladies of the night, while not as numerous, have extended their working hours, and men – especially Japanese – can expect to be accosted here even in the middle of the day.

IOLANI PALACE

Hawaii's "Merrie Monarch," King Kalakaua, was preoccupied with Europe's royal traditions, and in 1879 he instructed work to start on the Iolani Palace. It took three years to complete. The palace was filled with fine European furniture, much of it shipped round Cape Horn or painstakingly reproduced by local artisans. Following Kalakaua's death in 1891, Queen Liliuokalani lived in the palace until the 1893 coup that toppled the monarchy forever. The palace then served as Hawaii's seat of government until the new State Capitol (see page 50) was completed in 1969.

Several million dollars have been spent on the restoration of America's only royal palace, and it is now open to the public. As this is one of the most popular attractions on the island, reservations are highly recommended.

The grounds of the palace shouldn't be ignored. On the left of the main drive is the Coronation Bandstand, which King Kalakaua built for his coronation in 1883. He was the only monarch to be crowned here. It is now used for weddings, gubernatorial inaugurations and, every Friday at noon, a free concert by the Royal Hawaiian Band. Behind the palace stands a pair of banyan trees reputedly planted by Queen Kapiolani. *South King and Richards Streets. Tel: (808) 522–0832. Open: Wednesday to Saturday 9am–2:15pm. Tours leave every 15 minutes and last 45 minutes. No children under five admitted. Admission charge.*

KAPIOLANI PARK

At the foot of Diamond Head, on the edge of Waikiki, lies Hawaii's first public park. King Kalakaua gave these 220 acres to the people of Honolulu, asking that the park be named after his wife. Although many major tourist attractions are sited in the park, it remains a place where locals go for recreation. *Located at the eastern end of Kalakaua Avenue. Open: permanently. Free. Individual attractions within the park are listed separately.*

Curving palm trees in Kapiolani Park

KAWAIAHA'O CHURCH

This was the first Christian church in the Hawaian Islands. It was completed in 1842, built from coral blocks by its Hawaiian congregation. At one time, congregations of over 4,000 Hawaiians would gather here. It is still an active church today, although a visitor is more likely to witness a Japanese wedding ceremony than a Christian service.
Punchbowl Street at South King Street. Tel: (808) 522–1333. Open: daily 9am–4pm.

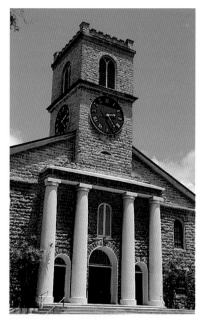

The Islands' monarchs were crowned and buried here at Kawaiaha'o Church

KING KAMEHAMEHA I STATUE

Honolulu's most important statue, standing in front of Aliiolani Hale, is but a replica – the original stands, larger than life, in front of the courthouse at Kapaau, a tiny town on the Big Island's north Kohala Coast (see page 106). On Kamehameha Day, every June, *leis* cover the outstretched arms of the statue.
417 South King Street.

KODAK HULA SHOW

Since 1937 this touristic version of Hawaii has been presented three times a week to 3,000 people, who often line up for the privilege of watching other tourists make fools of themselves doing the *hula*. However tacky the show may be, it is undeniably one of the best crowd-pullers in Kapiolani Park. A free shuttle serves major Waikiki hotels.
Opposite Honolulu Zoo. Tel: (808) 833–1661. Open: Tuesday to Thursday 10am–11:15am. Free.

KUAN YIN TEMPLE

Immediately adjacent to the Foster Botanical Garden (see page 42) is a masterpiece of Chinese architecture. This Taoist temple is dominated by a 10-foot statue of Kuan Yin, Buddhist goddess of mercy, surrounded by the usual eclectic assortment of shrines and artifacts found in traditional Chinese temples. Tours are available on request.
170 Vineyard Boulevard. Tel: (808) 533–6361. Open: daily 8:30am–2pm. Free.

LYON ARBORETUM

In the wet foothills of the interior – at the other end of the Manoa Valley from the University of Hawaii – the rainfall exceeds 160 inches a year. For an arboretum with hundreds of exotic tropical plants, such conditions are perfect. Its 124 acres are only a short drive from downtown Honolulu.
3860 Manoa Road. Tel: (808) 988–3177. Open: Monday to Saturday 9am–3pm. Closed: state holidays. Donation appreciated.

Kuan Yin Temple's green-tile roof covers an ornate interior perfumed with incense

MISSION HOUSES MUSEUM

In 1820 a group of Americans sailed to Honolulu to establish Hawaii's first Christian mission. In 20 years they established 17 missions throughout the Islands and taught 75 percent of the population to read in their own language.

The three historic houses that make up the Mission Houses Museum are the oldest remaining houses in the Islands. They are completely restored and furnished and provide a unique look at the encounter between American Protestant missionaries and native Hawaiians in the early 1800s.

The Mission Frame House is the focal point for guided tours. It is filled with the personal belongings of the Reverend Hiram Bingham and his wife, who lived here for 20 years. There is also the rocking chair of Queen Kaahumanu, who converted to Christianity and proclaimed the Ten Commandments to be the law of the kingdom. The Printing Office, home of the original Mission

Press, was instrumental in preserving the Hawaiian language. The press still works, and demonstrations are given daily. Chamberlain House was the home of Levi Chamberlain, the storekeeper. It was built from coral cut from the reef in 1831.

553 South King Street. Tel: (808) 531–0481. Open: Tuesday to Saturday 9am–4pm, Sunday noon–4pm (access to Frame House and Printing Office by guided tour only, every hour). Admission charge.

MOUNT TANTALUS

Puowaina Drive, the road to the Punchbowl Crater (see page 48), turns into Tantalus Drive and winds upward through exclusive housing on the slopes of Mount Tantalus. Panoramic views greet you at numerous points along the way. At the top the name changes to Round Top Drive and the road descends via Puu Ualakaa Park, which provides one of the best views of the city in all Honolulu.

Mission Houses Museum: costumed actors portray historical characters on Saturdays

The Columbia Memorial honors servicemen missing in action from World War II, Korea and Vietnam

NEAL S BLAISDELL CENTER

Neal Blaisdell was a popular mayor of Honolulu from 1955 to 1968. The 8,000-seat arena named for him is the main venue for major indoor sports events from basketball to sumo wrestling. It is also used for conventions, rock concerts and even circuses. The adjoining 2,158-seat concert hall is home to the Honolulu Symphony Orchestra. Major theatrical performances and ballet are also staged here. (See pages 150 and 158.)

777 Ward Avenue. Tel: (808) 521–2911. Open: see calendar of events.

PUNCHBOWL CRATER

Punchbowl refers to the shape of Puowaina ("Hill of Human Sacrifices"), the crater of an extinct volcano covering 116 acres. Always considered a sacred place by Hawaiians, in 1949 it was transformed into the National Memorial Cemetery of the Pacific.

The green, landscaped lawns covering the crater floor contain the graves of 33,143 American servicemen. The site is dominated by the Honolulu Memorial. A flight of steps leads up to a massive 30-foot statue of a female figure known as *Columbia*. On either side of the statue are maps recording the involvement of American forces in the Central and South Pacific regions and in Korea.

To the left of the Memorial, the road winds up to an overlook giving superb views of Honolulu out to Diamond Head. Vehicles can't drive to the lookout, but it's only a 10-minute walk from the parking lot.
2177 Puowaina Drive. Tel: (808) 566–1430. Open: daily 8am–5:30pm, 30 September to 1 March; 8am–6:30pm, March 2nd to September 29th, 7am–7pm Memorial Day. Free.

QUEEN EMMA SUMMER PALACE
Queen Emma, born in 1836, was one of the earliest symbols of Hawaii's cosmopolitan culture, being descended from both Hawaiian chieftains and Englishman John Young, who befriended Kamehameha the Great. Queen Emma was the wife of King Kamehameha IV, and this modest "palace" was her mountain home. The unpretentious wooden building has only two bedrooms and no guest quarters and stands on lovely grounds about five minutes from the center of Honolulu. The Palace, now a museum filled with paintings and furniture, has a distinctly British feel, perhaps as a result of Kamehameha's friendship with Queen Victoria.
2913 Pali Highway (just off the highway). Tel: (808) 595–3167. Open: daily 9am–4pm. Admission charge.

QUEEN KAPIOLANI GARDEN
Located behind the Honolulu Zoo in Kapiolani Park (see page 44), this poorly tended garden has obviously seen better days. None of the plants are labeled and the garden has little to interest the visitor, but it can at least offer a peaceful refuge from the frenzy of Waikiki.

QUEEN LILIUOKALANI STATUE
Liliuokalani was the sister of King Kalakaua, and when he died in San Francisco in 1891 she succeeded him to the Hawaiian throne. She tried to restore the power of the monarchy which her brother had signed away, but this led to a clash with business leaders and the downfall of the royal family. Her statue stands by a massive banyan tree behind the Iolani Palace (see page 45).

Queen Emma's summer retreat from royal pomp

ST ANDREW'S CATHEDRAL

King Kamehameha IV converted to the Church of England (whose trappings he admired) after the death of his four-year-old son. In 1858 he and his wife, Queen Emma, founded the Anglican Church of Hawaii and decided to build a cathedral. Construction began in 1867 under the direction of his widow, for the King had died four years earlier, on St Andrew's Day. The style of architecture is French Gothic, and the church was actually shipped piecemeal from England. The striking stained-glass window above the entrance depicts momentous events and personages in Hawaii's history, including the first bishop, the Reverend Thomas Staley, sent by Queen Victoria.
Queen Emma Square. Tel: (808) 524–2822. Open: daily 6:30am–6pm.

SKYGATE

In 1977, when Isamu Noguchi's black, 24-foot steel sculpture was unveiled, it provoked the usual criticisms directed at "modern art." Now, almost 20 years later, it's an established part of the downtown landscape.
Off South King Street.

STATE CAPITOL

Until 1969 the State Legislature was housed in the Iolani Palace. The new State Capitol, immediately behind the palace, symbolizes the state of Hawaii. Its palm trees are echoed in the columns, the sea is represented by the reflecting pool, and volcanoes by the conical rooms of the Legislature. In the inner courtyard is a 600,000-tile mosaic by Tadashi Sato, and on the Beretania Street side is a controversial statue by Marisol Escubar of Father Damien (see page 39), his originally handsome features distorted by leprosy.

Visitors can sit in on sessions of the Senate and House of Representatives from January to April.
South Beretania Street, Punchbowl and Richards Streets. Tel: (808) 548–2211. Open: Monday to Friday 8am–4:30pm; courtyard open 24 hours. Closed: state holidays.

Bishop Staley stands beside the King and Queen in St Andrew's hand-blown stained glass

THOMAS SQUARE

Flanked by the Honolulu Academy of Art and the Academy Art Center, this beautiful landscaped square appropriately hosts an arts and crafts fair every Sunday.

WAIKIKI AQUARIUM

Founded in 1904, this is America's third oldest public aquarium, reopened in 1994 after a $3.1 million renovation project. Although limited in size, the aquarium more than makes up for it in the quality of its exhibits. The Seavisions Theater has both films and living displays of jellyfish. Four main galleries encompass the exotic sea life of the tropical Pacific – the origin of hundreds of species found in Hawaii – local marine habitats, environmental concerns and threatened species and habitats. The 35,000-gallon Damon Shark Gallery is the centerpiece. At the far end is a miniature re-creation of a living coral reef.

Outside is a Hawaiian monk seal habitat, which simulates the primary natural habitat for these endangered creatures. Opposite is a *mahimahi* hatchery and nursery deck and an aquaculture exhibit, featuring adult and juvenile *mahimahi*, eggs and the food web cultivated to feed the young fish. Overlooking the ocean is the Edge of the Reef, a re-creation of the rocky Hawaiian shoreline. Children are encouraged to touch the marine life and learn about this special environment from interpretative staff.
2777 Kalakaua Avenue, between Waikiki Beach and Diamond Head. Tel: (808) 923–9741. Open: daily 9am–5pm. Closed: Thanksgiving and Christmas. Admission charge. Note: parking is very difficult. It is far better to take a no. 2 bus to Waikiki–Kapiolani Park.

A rare monk seal surfaces playfully in his simulated habitat at Waikiki Aquarium

WAR MEMORIAL NATATORIUM

See page 63.

WASHINGTON PLACE

This elegant mansion next to St Andrew's Cathedral is the residence of the Governor of Hawaii. It was originally built in 1846 by a sea captain who was subsequently lost at sea. His son, John Dominis, married Lydia Kapaakea, who eventually became Queen Liliuokalani. When she was deposed in 1893, after the death of Dominis, she returned from the Iolani Palace to Washington Place, where she lived until her death in 1917.
South Beretania Street, opposite the State Capitol. No public tours.

WIZARD STONES

Also known as the Kahuna Stones (see page 63).

Oahu

BYODO-IN TEMPLE

On a rainy day it's easy to imagine you're in Uji, Japan, where the original model for this temple was built over 900 years ago. The red wooden structure is set against green mountains, and the whole area has an aura of great serenity. It was built in 1968 to honour Hawaii's first Japanese immigrants, who had arrived 100 years before. The approach is

through a large park, and the temple does not come into view until you reach the parking lot immediately in front.
47–200 Kahekili Highway, Kaneohe. Tel: (808) 239–8811. Open: daily 9am–4pm. Admission charge.

DOLE PLANTATION
Central Oahu is still dominated by rolling fields of pineapples, and the Dole Plantation cashes in on this once important industry. A self-guided tour of the pineapple garden shows the varieties of pineapple from round the world, but the heart of the operation is the shop with all the usual souvenirs, pineapple products and other foodstuffs, plus free pineapple juice!
64–1550 Kamehameha Highway, 3 miles past Wahiawa. Tel: (808) 621–8408. Open: daily 9am–5.30pm. Closed: Christmas. Free.

HALONA BLOWHOLE
Waves crashing through a lava tube create this geyser-like spout of water, set against a spectacular backdrop of the islands of Molokai and Lanai.
Off Kalanianaole Highway, east of Hanauma Bay.

KOKO CRATER BOTANIC GARDEN
The hot, dry interior of the extinct Koko Crater provides 200 acres of ideal environment for desert plants, including cacti, aloes, euphorbias and sansevierias. Koko Crater is still in the early stages of development, but is a perfect complement to the other Honolulu Botanical Gardens.
Kealahou Street, off Kalanianaole Highway by Sandy Beach. Tel: (808) 522–7060. Open: daily 9am–4pm. Closed: Christmas and New Year's. Free.

Mist-shrouded peaks back the tranquil Temple

Dole-ful expression for pineapple lovers

MORMON TEMPLE
The town of Laie on the Windward Coast is 95 percent Mormon. Brigham Young University is located here next to the Polynesian Cultural Center, and down the road is the most visited Mormon temple outside Salt Lake City. The temple, built in 1919, can be glimpsed as you drive by on the main Kamehameha Highway. Visitors are not allowed to enter the temple but are welcome to wander round the grounds.
55–600 Naniloa Loop, off Kamehameha Highway. Tel: (808) 293–9297. Grounds open: daily 9am–8pm. Free.

NUUANU PALI LOOKOUT
The Lookout is signposted off the Pali Highway, and there is no better view of the windward side of Hawaii than from this windy spot. A short drive to the parking lot is followed by a short walk to the Lookout.

PACIFIC WHALING MUSEUM
This is the largest collection of whaling artifacts and scrimshaw in the Pacific. It is part of Sea Life Park (see page 56) but is entered through a separate gate next to the main park entrance.
Off Kalanianaole Highway, southeast of Waimanalo Bay. Tel: (808) 259–7933. Open: daily 9:30am–5pm. Free.

The theme-park approach to Pacific cultures provides entertainment and education at PCC

visitors along a meandering waterway to the different island re-creations. Tours on foot are another option. There is also a shuttle that leaves for different attractions throughout the day (make sure that it's going to your desired destination).

Different presentations are given throughout the day. Most visitors try to see the Pageant of the Long Canoes (2pm and 3pm). An Imax theater, seven storys high and 96 feet wide, screens a breathtakingly realistic *Polynesian Odyssey*, on the history and culture of Polynesia. Every evening at 7:30 a Polynesian spectacular called *Mana* is presented, featuring over 100 performers, cascading waterfalls and even an erupting volcano. This may sound more like Las Vegas than Polynesia, but the show never fails to satisfy audiences – even if some of the "Polynesian" performers are blond-haired and blue-eyed.

The Center has several snack bars and a restaurant serving buffet-style meals. There is an attempt at a *luau* which falls a long way short of a real *luau* experience, both in terms of food and atmosphere. In accordance with Mormon beliefs, alcohol is not served.

The staff are genuinely friendly and interested in sharing their knowledge of the South Pacific. In spite of its Mormon roots, there is no proselytizing. Package tours to the Center are available at most hotels.

POLYNESIAN CULTURAL CENTER

Far out of Honolulu on the Windward Coast, Brigham Young University and the Mormon Church have developed one of Hawaii's biggest and most polished tourist attractions. On a 42-acre site there are re-creations of villages from seven of Polynesia's main island groups. The inhabitants are BYU students who hail from those islands, including Samoa, Hawaii, the Marquesas, Tonga, New Zealand, Tahiti and Fiji. The theme-park approach to cultural anthropology works quite well and is certainly entertaining if somewhat sterile.

Double-hulled canoes transport

55–370 Kamehameha Highway, Laie. Tel: (808) 293–3333. Open: Monday to Saturday 12:30–9pm. Closed: Christmas and Thanksgiving. Admission charge. Bus no. 52 from Ala Moana Center.

PUU-O-MAHUKA HEIAU
STATE MONUMENT
The original _heiau_ (temple) has all but disappeared, though the view of the North Shore and Waimea Bay makes the visit well worthwhile. Human sacrifice here included three unfortunate English sailors in 1794.
After Waimea, take Pupukea Road east off the Kamehameha Highway and look for the red-and-yellow sign of the Hawaii Visitors Bureau.

ROYAL HAWAIIAN SHRIMP
AND PRAWN
At the far northern tip of Oahu, along an otherwise uninteresting stretch of road, cars line up by a little roadside stand that sells fresh prawns and shrimps straight out of the lagoons of the aquaculture farm behind it. This is a unique opportunity to see the biggest farm of its kind in the Islands, and also to savor some of the freshest seafood you'll ever find.
Kamehameha Highway, between Kahuku and Turtle Bay Hilton.

SCHOFIELD BARRACKS
The US Army's 25th Infantry Division headquarters are considered to be the most beautiful military base in the nation. A sign at the gate states "Home of the Infantry, Tropic Lightening." The Tropic Lightening Museum houses _memorabilia_ dating back to 1812, together with World War II planes, armaments from the Korean War and _pungi_ traps from Vietnam. The site allows a glimpse of what life is like on a major military installation.
McComb Gate, off Highway 99 past Wahiawa. Tel: (808) 655–0438. Open: Tuesday to Saturday 10am–4pm. Free. Tours of Schofield Barracks, together with the other major military bases on Oahu, are given by Top Gun Tours, PO Box 25204, Honolulu, HI 96825. Tel: (808) 396–8112.

Visitors' offerings at Puu-o-Mahuka Heiau

Sea life with a watery perspective at Hawaii's one-of-a-kind Sea Life Park

SEA LIFE PARK

Stunningly set on Makapuu Point, on the easternmost tip of Oahu, the park is home to a diverse collection of over 4,000 marine creatures of the Pacific, including the world's only living "wholphin" – a cross between an Atlantic bottlenose dolphin and a whale. In addition to the customary displays of fish from the surrounding oceans, there is a penguin habitat with a breeding colony of endangered Humboldt penguins. The highlight of Sea Life Park is a 300,000-gallon Hawaiian Reef tank, where you can take an intimate look at life beneath the surface.

Marine mammal shows feature dolphins performing in the Hawaiian Ocean Theater and Whaler's Cove, and a predictably corny review stars a troop of talented sea lions.

On a more serious level, the park includes the Hawaiian Monk Seal Care Center, which cares for stranded and injured monk seals, one of the world's most endangered marine mammals. *Makapuu Point, Waimanalo. Tel: (808) 259–7933. Open: daily 9:30am–5pm, Friday 9:30am–10pm. Admission charge. For free transportation from major hotels, tel: 923–3474.*

SENATOR FONG'S PLANTATION AND GARDENS

US Senator Hiram Fong started his 725-acre garden almost 40 years ago, and since his retirement in 1976 he has devoted much of his time to its cultivation. The gardens are more like a wild tropical rain forest than the neatly manicured flower beds of Europe. Because of the extent of the grounds, walking tours are impractical. Shuttle tours lasting about two hours leave from the gift shop.

47–285 Pulama Road, off Highway 83, Kahaluu. Tel: (808) 239–6775. Open: daily 10am–4pm. Tours at 10:30 and 11:30am, 1, 2 and 3pm. Admission charge.

S. MATSUMOTO STORE

The North Shore of Oahu is old Hawaii, both geographically and culturally distant from Waikiki. The small town of Haleiwa now has a growing number of arts and crafts stores, but there are still little gems to be found – like the funky old store of S. Matsumoto, famous throughout Hawaii for "shave ice." This local delicacy consists of finely shaven ice flavored with one of various syrups and served in a simple paper cone. Matsumoto's makes its own syrups, which makes all the difference. Even if you're not tempted by a delicious, refreshing shave ice after a hard day at the beach, the place is still worth visiting to see a way of life that no longer exists in most of Oahu.

66–087 Kamehameha Highway, Haleiwa. Tel: (808) 637–4827. Open: daily 8:30am–5:30pm.

WAIMEA FALLS PARK

The only major visitor attraction on the North Shore of Oahu is the 1,800 acres of Waimea Falls Park. The Waimea Valley was the home of Oahu's priests from about A.D.1092, and centuries later the valley was bestowed upon the high priest of King Kamehameha the Great. Many of the ancient sites in the park have been excavated and supplemented

with living history exhibits, ranging from Hawaiian games to sacred practices.

The park is primarily a botanical garden. Walking is the best way to see it all, but there is a free open-air shuttle round the sites which includes a full narration of the main features. Taking the shuttle up to the falls and walking back down is the ideal compromise.

Four times a day, professional divers demonstrate their skills in a 30-minute show at the 55-foot Waimea Falls, at the far end of the park. Other demonstrations include the *hula* and wildlife feeding.

59–864 Kamehameha Highway, across from Waimea Bay Beach Park, Haleiwa. Tel: (808) 638 8511. Open: daily 10am–5:30pm. Admission charge.

A five-story plunge at Waimea Falls Park

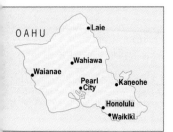

OAHU

- Laie
- Wahiawa
- Waianae
- Pearl City
- Kaneohe
- Honolulu
- Waikiki

Chinatown

The Chinese first arrived in Hawaii in the mid-1800s, and in the ensuing years Chinatown developed into one of the biggest neighborhoods in the city. Fires twice destroyed the area, in 1886 and again in 1900, so all the buildings featured on this walk date from after this period. *Allow 2 hours.*

Street parking in Chinatown can be very difficult to find. The best place to start the walk is by the Aloha Tower, where there are 4-hour parking meters. From here it is only a few minutes' walk into Chinatown. Begin the walk at the corner of Kekaulike Street and North King Street.

1 OAHU MARKET

This covered market, established in 1904, is the perfect introduction to the smells and tastes of the Orient.
Turn right into North King Street and left into Maunakea Street.

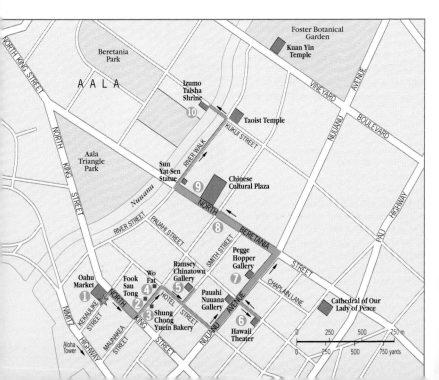

A taste of old China transplanted to the US

2 FOOK SAU TONG
The shop at 1016 Maunakea Street has a bizarre window display of dusty old snakes, dried seahorses and other weird items associated with Chinese herbal medicine.
Cross the street to no 1027.

3 SHUNG CHONG YUEIN BAKERY
This establishment not only offers a huge selection of Chinese delicacies, but also has a colorful shrine in the back of the shop, complete with burning joss sticks.
Continue to the corner of Hotel Street.

4 WO FAT RESTAURANT
Reputed to be the oldest restaurant in Honolulu, if not the state, this landmark site has been in business since 1882, though the present building dates from 1937. It makes an ideal lunch stop.
Turn right into Hotel Street and left into Smith Street.

5 RAMSEY CHINATOWN GALLERY
The gallery at 1128 Smith Street has regular shows of major artists working in the Islands. It's housed in the 1923 Tan Sing building.
Return to Hotel Street, turn left and left again into Nuuanu Avenue. Turn right down Pauahi Street to the corner.

6 HAWAII THEATER
Although now in a sad state of repair, this was once the largest center for the performing arts in the state.
Return along Pauahi Street and turn right into Nuuanu Avenue.

7 PEGGE HOPPER GALLERY
The gallery's two floors are devoted to the work of Hawaii's best-known living painter. On show, and for sale, is a wide diversity of Hopper's work, from fluid nude studies to highly stylized portraits.
Continue along Nuuanu Avenue to North Beretania Street and turn left.

8 NORTH BERETANIA STREET
The block past Smith Street has several *lei* shops where you can watch these elaborate flower garlands being made. The Lau family, who run Sweetheart's Lei Shop at 79A Beretania, have been in business for almost 60 years.
Cross Beretania Street and walk left towards River Walk.

9 CHINESE CULTURAL PLAZA
A statue of Sun Yat Sen, the father of the Chinese Republic, stands next to the Chinese Cultural Plaza, where performances are often given on the open Moongate Stage. At any time of day there may be a group of people on stage practising tai-chi movements. Surrounding the stage are several Chinese shops and restaurants.
Turn right into River Walk to Kukui Street. Turn left.

10 IZUMO TAISHA SHRINE
This Shinto shrine built in 1923 was confiscated in World War II and not returned to its congregation until 1962. The giant bags of rice near the altar symbolize good health.
Return to the Aloha Tower.

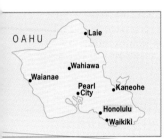

OAHU

•Laie

•Wahiawa

•Waianae

Pearl •Kaneohe
•City

•Honolulu

•Waikiki

Historic Honolulu

Downtown Honolulu is an eclectic mix of venerable old buildings and new high-rise offices. This walk introduces you to most of the district's historic sites, and also offers a glimpse of everyday Honolulu. You will find few souvenir shops and tourist restaurants here. This is office-worker territory! *Allow 90 minutes, plus time to visit museums.*

Start at the Hawaii Maritime Center. The parking lot is rarely full, and it has 4-hour and 8-hour parking meters.

1 FALLS OF CLYDE
The *Falls of Clyde* served variously as a cargo vessel, passenger ship and oil tanker from 1878 to 1959. It's now a floating museum moored alongside the Hawaii Maritime Center (see page 43).
Continue along the seafront.

2 ALOHA TOWER
This is the best-known building in all Honolulu, the Hawaiian equivalent of New York City's Statue of Liberty (see page 32). Since 1926 the Tower has been the first sight to greet seafarers heading for the Hawaiian Islands.
Walk up Bishop Street for two blocks to Queen Street.

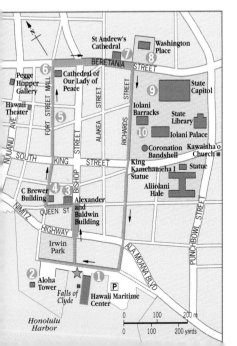

3 ALEXANDER AND BALDWIN BUILDING
Alexander and Baldwin, founded on the sugar industry in 1870, is one of Hawaii's most important companies. Its impressive headquarters have stood on the corner of Bishop and Queen Streets since 1929, and its design incorporates elements from just about every architectural influence in the world. Tile murals in the main entrance depict Hawaiian fish, and the ceiling is also decoratively tiled.
Turn left into Queen Street and walk to Fort Street on the next corner.

4 C BREWER BUILDING

This was the corporate headquarters of C Brewer & Co for almost 60 years. The company dates back to 1826 when James Hunnewell arrived in Honolulu with 40 barrels of goods from the mainland for sale. This fine Mediterranean-style building is on the National Register of Historic Places.
Continue up Fort Street and cross South King Street.

5 FORT STREET MALL

The street derives its name from a harbor-side fort built in 1816 and destroyed in 1857. The Mall is a pedestrian precinct lined with shops and cafés. At lunchtime it's crowded with officeworkers from the surrounding high-rise buildings and government offices.
Continue up the Mall towards Beretania Street.

6 CATHEDRAL OF OUR LADY OF PEACE

To the right, just before reaching Beretania, is the first Catholic church to be built in Hawaii. A group of Catholic missionaries arrived in Hawaii in 1827 but met a great deal of opposition from both the ruling chiefs and the Protestants. In 1837 they were banished but returned two years later when King Kamehameha III granted freedom of worship to his people. The missionaries began building this cathedral in 1843, and it was here in 1864 that Father Damien was ordained, before starting his legendary work on Molokai (see pages 39 and 130).
Turn right into Beretania, cross the street and walk two blocks to Alakea Street.

7 ST ANDREW'S CATHEDRAL

This Victorian-era church was shipped in pieces from England (see page 50).

8 WASHINGTON PLACE

The Governor's Mansion, next door to St Andrew's, is set back behind wrought-iron gates and an imposing drive (see page 51).
Cross Beretania Street into Richards Street.

9 STATE CAPITOL

Recently renovated to counter attacks from the elements, the State Capitol is designed on the theme of Hawaii (see page 50).
Continue down Richards Street.

10 IOLANI PALACE

Clearly inspired by Old World architecture, the former monarch's home is on the left (see page 45).
Return to the Maritime Center. If you have the time and energy, you can add a visit to that excellent museum at this point, feeding the parking meter as needed!

Tiled insets at Alexander and Baldwin Building

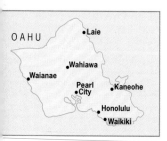

Waikiki

Waikiki was a mosquito-infested swampland until the Ala Wai Canal drained the land in the 1920s. The area became an exclusive luxury resort which Middle America discovered in the early 1960s – and then development proceeded in earnest! Waikiki, now the tourist heart of Honolulu, covers less than a square mile, but on any given day its beaches and streets can be crammed with over 100,000 people, making it one of the most densely populated areas on Earth. Well over half these people will be tourists; the rest are those who cater to them. This walk passes many of the most historically significant buildings of Waikiki. It is essentially a beach walk, so dress appropriately and take good sun protection. *Allow 90 minutes, plus time for visits.*

Start at Fort de Russy Beach, ¼ mile south of the Hilton Hawaiian Village.

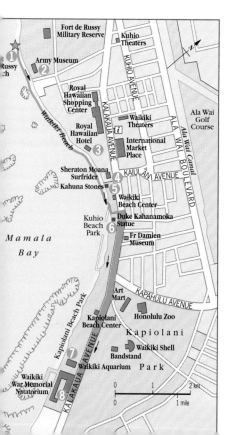

1 FORT DE RUSSY BEACH
Backed by a picturesque grove of palm trees, this is one of the widest and least crowed stretches of sand in Honolulu. It is owned by the US Army, which provides lifeguards and other essential facilities.

2 FORT DE RUSSY ARMY MUSEUM
Just inland from the beach, this museum is housed at Battery Randolph (see page 34).
Continue along the beach.

3 ROYAL HAWAIIAN HOTEL
Affectionately known as the Pink Palace, this elegant old hotel is now dwarfed by its neighbors, but when it was built in 1927 it dominated Waikiki. Here could be found the ultimate in luxury of every sort – where else did the fountains run with fresh pineapple juice? The hotel

The two-mile beach at Waikiki, with Diamond Head in the distance, invites a leisurely stroll

was patronized exclusively by the rich and famous: early Hollywood stars like Mary Pickford, Douglas Fairbanks and Al Jolson flocked over to Hawaii to stay here and rub shoulders with the Rockefellers, Duponts and European royalty.

Continue along the beach.

4 SHERATON MOANA SURFRIDER

This was the first hotel in Waikiki. Built in 1901, the white colonial-style architecture more than holds its own against the modern concrete buildings all around. It was here that Robert Louis Stevenson started work on *Treasure Island.* An enormous banyan tree in the hotel's courtyard provides welcome shade for midwalk refreshments.

5 KAHUNA STONES

On the beach just past the Moana Surfrider is a group of stones – often called the Wizard Stones of Waikiki – singularly ordinary and barely worth a second glance, sitting under a small tree. Yet they are believed to have been imbued with supernatural healing powers by four *kahunas* (priests) from Tahiti, who arrived in Hawaii during the 12th century. Most Hawaiians firmly believe in

the ancient mythology passed to them by oral tradition and they take these matters very seriously, so approach the stones respectfully.

Continue along the beach.

6 DUKE KAHANAMOKA STATUE

This monument on Kuhio Beach, which pays homage to the father of modern surfing, stands appropriately by racks of surfboards available for hire. Early every morning, the so-called Dawn Patrol can be seen "hanging ten" in the surf here as if in daily tribute to the Duke.

Leave the beach and walk along Kalakaua Avenue towards Kapiolani Park.

7 WAIKIKI AQUARIUM

See page 51.

8 WAR MEMORIAL NATATORIUM

Adjacent to the Aquarium is this saltwater swimming pool, built in 1927 as a World War I memorial. It has fallen into serious disrepair, and arguments still rage over whether it should be restored. Its murky waters are best avoided.

Either walk back along the beach or go over to Kuhio Avenue for a bus or taxi back to the Hilton Hawaiian Village.

Kauai

*I*t is not without reason that Kauai is called the Garden Isle. Lush is an understatement for this tropical Eden. Of all the islands, Kauai comes closest to most people's image of a South Pacific paradise – so much so that it frequently substitutes for the real thing in Hollywood films (see pages 70–1).

A prerequisite for this extravagant beauty is rain, and lots of it. Mount Waialeale, 5,150 feet (1,569m), in central Kauai, has an annual rainfall of over 450 inches – the heaviest on earth. Rarely does a day pass without rain falling somewhere on Kauai, but the island is so small – a mere 33 miles at its widest point – that sunshine is only a short drive away. The Kayo area has the most consistently sunny weather.

Kauai is one of the quietest and most rural of the islands. There is no big town, only three big resort hotels, and two of those are appropriately sedate and tasteful. Nightlife is virtually non-existent.

Where Kauai excels is in the host of activities that complement its dramatic and widely varied scenery. These range from hiking to kayaking to horseback riding. The island also boasts the finest restaurant in all Hawaii, incongruously located in a Kapaa shopping center. A Pacific Café is easily the equal of the very best restaurants found on the mainland.

Kauai is the most westerly of the main islands, making it vulnerable not only to rain but also hurricanes. In 1982 and 1992, devastating hurricanes, accompanied by massive tidal waves, caused millions of dollars' worth of damage and closed hotels for several months. With remarkable resilience the island was up and running again within a year. Vegetation has grown back and buildings have been reconstructed. The first-time visitor wouldn't suspect there had ever been a problem.

Left: taro fields cover Kauai's landscape
Right: a gentle sea beckons in a secluded spot

KAUAI

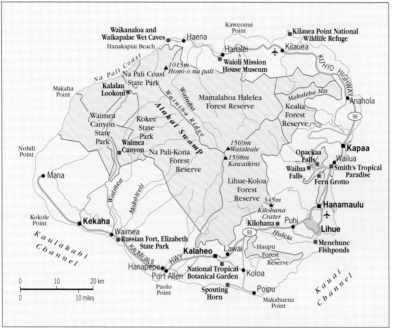

Kaweonui Point

Waikanaloa and
Waikapalae Wet Caves

Haena

Hanakapiai Beach

Na Pali Coast

Kilauea Point National
Wildlife Refuge

Hanalei

Kilauea

Waioli Mission
House Museum

1015m
Hono o na pali

KUHIO HIGHWAY

Makaha
Point

Kalalau
Lookout

Na Pali Coast
State Park

Waininha Ridge

Mamalahoa Halelea
Forest Reserve

Makaleha Mts

Anahola

Waimea
Canyon
State
Park

Kokee
State
Park

Alakai Swamp

Kealia
Forest
Reserve

56

Nohili
Point

Waimea
Canyon

Na Pali-Kona
Forest
Reserve

1569m
Waialeale
▲*1598m*
Kawaikini

Opaekaa
Falls

Kapaa

Wailua

Smith's Tropical
Paradise

Mana

Waimea

Makaweli

Lihue-Koloa
Forest
Reserve

Wailua
Falls

Fern Grotto

Kokole
Point

Kekaha

*Kaulakahi
Channel*

Waimea
Russian Fort, Elizabeth
State Park

KAUMUALII

345m
*Kilohana
Crater*

Kilohana

Puhi

50

Huleia

Hanamaulu

Lihue

Menehune
Fishponds

Kalaheo

Lawai

Haupu
Forest
Reserve

Hanapepe
Port Allen

HWY

National Tropical
Botanical Garden

Koloa

*Kauai
Channel*

Puolo
Point

Spouting
Horn

Poipu

Makahuena
Point

0   10   20 km

0   10 miles

Like young green stalactites, the hanging foliage at Fern Grotto covers the rock face

chanting, dancing the *hukelau* and such. The river trip alone would make the excursion worthwhile.

It is a short, but often wet, walk from the boat landing to the grotto. Usually there are continuous boatloads of people going in, and each group has to listen to the *Hawaiian Wedding Song* performed by the crew – which can cause backlogs, particularly irritating when it is raining!

Two tours operate out of Wailua Marina; both operate daily 9am–4pm. *Smith's Motor Boat Service. Tel: (808) 822-4111.*
Waialeale Boat Tours. Tel: (808) 822-4908.

GROVE FARM HOMESTEAD

Eighty acres of beautifully landscaped gardens surround the Grove Farm Homestead on the outskirts of Lihue. It is so uncommercialized that people are almost discouraged from visiting the site. Reservations must be made well in advance (drop-in visitors will be turned away), and only six people are allowed per tour to minimize wear and tear on the buildings. But do make the effort. The homestead, built by George Wilcox, a missionary's son, dates from 1864 and is typical of the old sugar plantations. It was a going concern until the mid-1930s when Wilcox died.

Located off Nawiliwili Road, Lihue (precise directions given when making reservations). Tel: (808) 245-3202. Open: Monday, Wednesday and Thursday for tours at 10am and 1pm. Reservations can be made by telephone or by writing (up to 3 months in advance) to: Grove Farm Homestead, PO Box 1631, Lihue, Kauai, HI 96766. Admission charge.

FERN GROTTO

There are certain places where locals never venture, and this is one of them. On Kauai this is the closest there is to a tourist trap. The grotto is really quite beautiful, although recent storm and hurricane damage has destroyed many of the ferns that drape down from the roof 40 feet above.

The only way to reach the grotto is by boat along the Wailua River. The Wailua is the only navigable river in Hawaii, and this unique journey passes through incomparable scenery – though you may be distracted from it by the forced merriment of sing-along Hawaiian

HANALEI

"Puff the Magic Dragon lived by the sea and frolicked in the autumn mists in a land called Hanalei" – and here it is. Puff may no longer be around, but the magic remains. Hanalei is a one-street town of clapboard houses and shops that look like they've been here forever. A backdrop of steep, verdant cliffs completes the picture. Visiting this Hawaiian backwater, a gathering point for surf bums and dropouts, is like time-warping back to the 1960s. The aroma of illegal substances hangs in the air and life passes by at a relaxed pace.

The Hanalei Valley Lookout, high above the town on the road to Princeville, surveys a patchwork of taro fields cut by the Hanalei River and framed by cliffs soaring to 3,500 feet. It is also the site of the 917-acre Hanalei National Wildlife Refuge, home to the Hawaiian gallinule, the Hawaiian stilt and many other water birds. There is free access to the reserve, although much of it is under water or planted with taro. Enter from Ohiki Road, which runs into the old bridge directly below the Lookout.

HANAPEPE

This town, near the main highway, is worth the short detour to see a typical tin-roof plantation town complete with wooden sidewalks and old false-front stores.

Just before reaching the town you'll see the Hanapepe Valley Lookout; stop to take in the steep gorge of Hanapepe Valley, heavily carpeted with native plants.

Dark cliffs behind, half-moon beach in front: Hanalei leaves a mystical memory

KALALAU LOOKOUT

The best way to experience the Na Pali Coast of Kauai is up close and on foot, but the next best thing is the view from the Kalalau Lookout. The only effort involved is the drive from sea level to 4,000 feet. A long, steep road winds up through Kokee State Park to the road head, and only a few short steps will take you from the car park to the view point. A trail leading up towards Mount Waialeale gives great views across the valley. Try to get up here before 10am, if possible, because clouds roll in almost every afternoon and obliterate the incredible view, which is particularly galling after the long drive up.

Although no one lives in the valley now, until this century it was a thriving community supporting hundreds of Hawaiians. There are no trails down from the Lookout, but the valley can be reached by the difficult Kalalau Trail from the North Shore.

KAUAI MUSEUM

Lihue doesn't have much to offer tourists, but the little Kauai Museum is a treasure house of Hawaiiana. This former library has two main areas: in the main building are exhibits on the ethnic heritage of the island, and in the adjacent building are natural history exhibits. Even an hour spent in the museum will give you a good solid background on Kauai.
4428 Rice Street, Lihue. Tel: (808) 245–6931. Open: Monday to Friday 9.am–4:30pm, Saturday 9:30am–1pm. Admission charge.

Above: Kauai Museum

KILAUEA POINT NATIONAL WILDLIFE REFUGE

Steep sea cliffs attract a diverse range of resident and migrating birds to this refuge. The rugged heights are a giant rookery for red-footed boobies, tropic birds and albatrosses. Great frigate birds can often be seen wheeling round in the sky.

On Kilauea Point itself is Kilauea Lighthouse, built in 1913 and now designated a National Historic Landmark. The clamshell lens is the biggest in the world, capable of sending a beam of light 90 miles out to sea. The Coast Guard stopped operating the light in 1967 when an automatic light was installed, and the whole 169-acre wildlife reserve is now operated by the US Fish and Game Service.

A small visitor center has been closed indefinitely for repairs, but the lookout is still open. From December to April this is a fine place to watch the migration of humpback whales.

KILOHANA

On the road from Lihue to Poipu, a grand Tudor-style mansion can be seen set back from the road. Built in 1935, the 16,000-square-foot house was once the home of the Wilcoxes, one of Kauai's most prominent families. Gaylord Wilcox was head of the Grove Farm Plantation and a relative of George Wilcox, who founded Grove Farm. Now it is a collection of craft shops, art galleries and a restaurant. The grounds are as interesting as the house and can be toured by carriage, while wagon tours go out into the cane fields.
Off Highway 50, Puhi. Tel: (808)

Cool, swirling cloud accompanies hikers on the mountainous trails of Kokee State Park

245–5608. Open: Monday to Saturday 9:30am–9:30pm, Sunday 9:30am–5pm. Free (not including carriage and wagon tours).

KOKEE STATE PARK

The park extends over 4,345 acres of lush wilderness complete with waterfalls, swimming holes and dramatic views. This is a nature-lover's paradise with its multitude of trails winding through a jungle of native plants and birds. The cool air at 4,000 feet is a welcome relief from the heat of the coast. The wise visitor carries rain gear.

The tiny Kokee Natural History Museum on Highway 550 is the best place to pick up trail information. It also has informative displays and videos on both Kokee State Park and Waimea Canyon.
End of Highway 550. Tel: (808) 335–9975. Open: daily 10am–4pm. Free.

Left: mariners' landmark, Kilauea Lighthouse
Right: Kilohana, a 1935 relic of elite island life

HAWAII AT THE MOVIES

A group of islands as scenic and spectacular as Hawaii was inevitably going to attract the attention of Hollywood. Tinseltown became hooked on Hawaii as early as 1913, when two one-reelers were made on Oahu – *Hawaiian Love* and *The Shark God*. Since then over 130 features have been made on the Islands.

Hawaii has primarily been used to provide a generic South Pacific location, although paradoxically the Islands are

Elvis Presley starring in one of his most famous movies, *Blue Hawaii*

north of the Equator. *South Pacific* may have been the title, but Mitzi Gaynor washed that man right out of her hair on Kauai's Lumahai Beach.

Many of the films made here are totally unmemorable apart from the scenery, but a few are worthy of mention.

Spencer Tracy braved the ocean off the Big Island in the Hemingway classic *The Old Man and the Sea*. Steve McQueen and Dustin Hoffman starred in *Papillon* (this time Hawaii was posing as the Caribbean).

It was at Kauai's Coco Palms Resort that Elvis hula'd his way through *Blue Hawaii*. The next year, 1962, he followed it with *Girls! Girls! Girls!* The rain forests of Kauai have seen the remake of *King Kong* with Jessica Lange and Jeff Bridges and, most recently, the prehistoric dinosaurs of *Jurassic Park*. *Raiders of the Lost Ark* was made here, as well as such diverse films as *Body Heat*, *Throw Momma From the Train* and *10*.

Honolulu has been a favourite home for private eyes since the days of Charlie Chan and his Number One Son. And the small-screen seems to have inherited a similar infatuation. *Hawaiian Eye* starring Robert Conrad and Connie Stevens was made here in the early 1960s. Throughout the 1970s, Jack Lord starred in *Hawaii 5-0*, and then came Tom Selleck in *Magnum PI*. The most recent Hawaiian private eye was the late William Conrad, starring in *Jake and the Fatman*.

MENEHUNE FISHPONDS

Every Hawaiian schoolchild learns that if anything goes wrong, they can blame it on the Menehune, a mythical race of little people, similar to leprechauns, who have lived on the Islands since long before the Polynesians arrived. Seldom seen and working only at night, they possess phenomenal physical strength, as evidenced by this waterway made out of hand-cut stones. It is unlike anything built in Polynesia and has long puzzled archaeologists. These industrious little people also created a huge 900-foot-long wall to cut off a bend in the Huleia Stream and thus form the Menehune or Alakopko Fishponds. What's more, they built it in a single night!

Menehune Ditch, Menehune Road, Waimea.
Menehune Fishponds, Niumalu Road just south of Lihue.

NA PALI COAST STATE PARK

The Na Pali Coast (see page 76) is one of the great natural sights of the world. For almost 600 years a small group of Hawaiians made their home in this awe-inspiring environment, where steep green cliffs plunge down towards the sea. A hike along the difficult Kalalau Trail (the sole access to the park) reveals the remains of their simple houses and ancient temples. You need a permit from the Department of Land and Natural Resources to hike past Hanakapiai Beach, two miles from the road head (tel: 808 241-3444).

NATIONAL TROPICAL BOTANICAL GARDEN

This 186-acre preserve is one of the finest gardens in Hawaii, dedicated to

Imperious, impenetrable: the Na Pali cliffs

the preservation of plants in danger of extinction. Every year up to 1,000 new plants are propagated here. Severe damage by Hurricane Iniki in 1992 closed the garden to the public, but restoration is progressing rapidly. The twice-daily tours have always been by appointment. Write for more information.

Box 340, Lawai, HI 96765. Tel: (808) 332–7361. Admission charge.

OLD KOLOA TOWN

This old sugar plantation town lies at the end of a famous tunnel of eucalyptus trees. Hurricane Iniki did its best to destroy the tunnel in 1992, but such is the fecundity of Kauai that the trees have almost grown back to their former glory. The town was restored in the 1980s, preserving the false-front buildings but adding new shops and restaurants behind the façades. The Koloa History Center, a tiny museum in Old Koloa Town Hall, displays a few plantation artifacts together with exhibits on local history.

Koloa History Center, junction of Highways 520 and 530 (no telephone). Open: daily 9am–5pm. Free.

OPAEKAA FALLS

Highway 580 leaves the main Kuhio Highway by Coco Palms in Wailua. It winds up steeply into a dramatic mountain landscape passing several ancient *heiau* (temple) sites on the way. An overlook on the right, soon after the road levels off, gives a grandstand view of the beautiful Opaekaa Falls.

POIPU

Before Hurricane Iniki struck in 1992, Poipu was a development of resort hotels and vacation homes along the sunny

Best observed in late afternoon, Poipu's Spouting Horn sounds like a breathing whale

southern coast of Kauai. The beaches were small compared to the North Shore, but the weather was a more than adequate compensation. Iniki devastated the area. Only one major resort has reopened, the Hyatt Regency. Poipu is gradually recovering, however, and enough facilities are operating to ensure a wonderful escape from the crowds. Surprisingly, the once skimpy beaches have grown, and beautiful stretches of golden sand have appeared where none existed before. Poipu's most famous feature is the Spouting Horn, a geyser-like fountain of seawater that regularly shoots into the air, caused by waves forced through an old lava tube.

Unable to adapt to grass huts, Waioli
missionaries built a New England-style home

RUSSIAN FORT, ELIZABETH STATE PARK

Once upon a time, a Russian fort with 38
guns and walls 30 feet thick stood on this
site at the entrance to Waimea. All that's
left is a heap of rubble and barely
identifiable foundations. There are a few
interpretative displays on the site, but the
best reason for visiting the park is the
commanding view of Waimea Bay, where
Captain Cook first landed in Hawaii.
*Highway 50, west of Waimea, just before
entering town. Always open.*

SMITH'S TROPICAL PARADISE

This commercial "paradise" occupies 30
acres at the mouth of the Wailua River. It
is from here that the boats operated by
the Smith family leave for Fern Grotto
(see page 66). The gardens are well-
stocked with both common and unusual
plants, and a series of plywood cut-out
"villages" suggest a mini theme park.
Mini-shuttles are available (for a small
fee) to transport the less mobile round
the gardens. The evening *luau* here is
reputedly the most popular on the island,
and features its own volcanic eruption.
Reservations are essential.
*Wailua Marina off Highway 56. Tel: (808)
822–4654. Open: daily 8.30am–4pm
(reopens for evening* luau*). Admission
charge.*

WAIKANALOA AND WAIKAPALAE WET CAVES

The location of these unremarkable
caves, adjoining the highway on the
dramatic North Shore, is the main reason
they're visited so frequently. People have
been known to swim in the murky water.
To the left of Highway 56.

POLIAHU HEIAU

Heiaus (temples) occur throughout
Hawaii, and most often they are now no
more than a pile of rocks. A square of
stones is all that's left of this one, which
was supposedly built by the mythical
Menehune (see page 72). Many
Hawaiians believe that ancestral spirits
dwell in the rocks, so please refrain from
walking on them. There are often small
rocks wrapped in *ti* leaves placed on the
walls, seemingly part of an authentic
ritual. In fact, they are placed there by
tourists who, for some unknown reason,
think it will bring good luck.

A path leads down from the *heiau* to
the Bell Stone; this was pounded after
the birth of a royal child, and its peal
would echo down the valley. By far the
most interesting aspect is the wonderful
view down the Wailua River valley.
*Just off Highway 580, before the Opaekaa
Falls turnoff.*

WAILUA FALLS

The road passes through three miles of sugar-cane fields before reaching the twin falls of Wailua. Hawaiian chiefs used to dive from the 80-foot cliff as a display of courage. Paths lead to both the top and bottom of the falls, but both are treacherous and may not be worth the risk. The overlook gives an excellent view of the waterfall and surrounding scenery. *Maalo Road off Highway 56, just before reaching Kapaa.*

WAIMEA CANYON

Mark Twain called this the Grand Canyon of the Pacific. An exaggeration, to be sure, but the 10-mile-long, 3,500-foot-deep canyon is nevertheless one of the great natural sights of Hawaii. A few trails venture down into the canyon, but more interesting hikes are afforded by Kokee State Park. The recommended road up to the canyon lookout hugs the canyon rim as it climbs to almost 4,000 feet. *Waimea Canyon Drive.*

WAIOLI MISSION HOUSE MUSEUM

Missionaries from New England brought over this house, in prefabricated sections, in 1836. Several different families lived here, but eventually the Wilcox family of Grove Farm fame (see page 66) became the permanent residents. The interior is filled with period furnishings, and the landscaped grounds are as interesting as the house. The house closed in 1992 after Hurricane Iniki; phone for current opening hours. *Highway 56, Hanalei. Tel: (808) 245–3202.*

Right: sightseeing on the Wailua River. Below: the Wet Caves were formed while under the sea

Na Pali Coast

In ancient times the remote Kalalau Valley on Kauai's North Shore was a thriving community and the steep, tortuous Kalalau Trail was the only access. The trail cuts across the precipitous Na Pali cliffs and clings perilously close to the edge. This is not only one of the greatest walks in Hawaii, but ranks among the greatest walks in the world. The entire Kalalau Trail is 11 miles long – a serious undertaking that should be attempted only by experienced backpackers, which requires an overnight camping stop. Fortunately the drama and splendour of this classic trail can be sampled with this day hike, which can be tailored according to the stamina and enthusiasm of the individual hiker. *Allow a full day.*

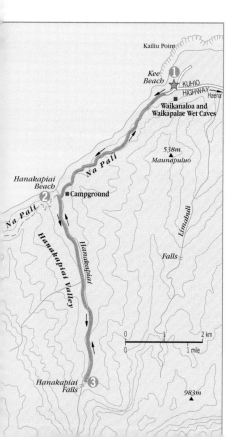

Take the Kuhio Highway as far as it will go. At the end is Kee Beach, where there is some off-road parking. During the morning this fills up, but there's a parking lot a few hundred yards down the road. The trail-head is well marked on the left-hand side of the road.

1 KEE BEACH

When the surf is gentle, this is one of the best swimming and snorkelling beaches on the North Shore, with a brilliantly colored coral reef packed with tropical fish. It provides the perfect way to relax after a strenuous day on the trail. The only facilities available are restrooms and showers.

Pass the trail-head map and sign-in box for overnight campers. Climb steeply for 1 mile. Looking back gives superb views of the North Shore and Kee Beach. The trail descends for another mile, even more steeply, back down to sea level. A stream crosses the path and, depending on the rainfall, it may be necessary to wade across to gain access to the beach.

Rugged terrain on the Na Pali Coast provides a challenging contrast to soft, sandy beaches

2 HANAKAPIAI BEACH

This beautiful stretch of sand is backed by the dramatic Na Pali cliffs. Because of its isolation, it's one of the few beaches in Hawaii where nude bathing is tolerated. During the winter months the sea here can be very dangerous and swimming is not advised.

Hanakapiai Beach itself is a worthwhile destination for a half-day hike from Kee Beach, but the hike up into Hanakapiai Valley to the falls will more than double the pleasure and satisfaction. The unmaintained trail climbs steeply, following the stream, passing old taro patches and mango trees.

For the first mile the trail is fairly well defined, but after crossing the stream it becomes increasingly difficult to follow. The last mile can be very hard, with several stream crossings, but if the stream is always kept in view, the falls will eventually come into sight.

BEWARE

Although there is no shortage of water on the trail, it is not necessarily fit for drinking. Most of the water is biologically contaminated and can cause unpleasant stomach problems. Carry a good, safe supply.

Mosquitoes here are vicious, and a strong insect repellent will prevent a lot of irritation.

3 HANAKAPIAI FALLS

The 300-foot falls plunge into a magnificent pool in a natural amphitheatre. The water provides a refreshing, if somewhat cool, spot for a swim after the strenuous hike up. Because of falling rocks and debris, it is safer not to swim directly under the falls.

Return by the same route to Kee Beach.

Maui

Maui is the second largest of the Hawaiian Islands, covering 729 square miles, and the second most popular tourist destination after Oahu. The island is divided into two distinctly shaped masses joined by a narrow neck of land. At the center of West Maui are the West Maui Mountains, while East Maui is dominated by the 10,000-foot dormant volcano, Haleakala. All the roads skirt these impenetrable geological formations – so, with over 2.5 million visitors a year, each with a rental car, traffic jams can be a serious problem.

Although the island is only 48 miles long and 26 miles across, it offers an extraordinarily wide range of attractions. Outdoor sports enthusiasts can participate in some of the best wind-surfing in Hawaii, horseback riding, and hiking in the world's biggest dormant volcano, in addition to world-class golf and tennis. Scenery extends from sun-drenched beaches to rain-drenched tropical forest; from lush valleys to moon-like volcanic landscapes.

MAUI, LANAI AND MOLOKAI

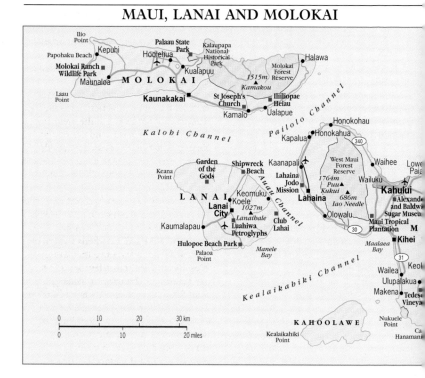

The Hana Coast's verdant cliffs and emerald sea

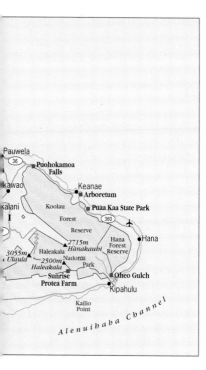

Accommodations follow the same principle, from luxury resorts to inexpensive self-catering condominiums and bed-and-breakfast inns.

West Maui is popular with younger visitors, the main attraction being the old whaling town of Lahaina, the only place on the island with any kind of night life. Kaanapali and Kapalua are lined with deluxe resort hotels where the beaches are blessed with sun even when the West Maui Mountains are deluged.

In East Maui the main resort areas are Kihei, Wailea and Makena. This stretch of coast also attracts good weather. The resorts at Wailea and Makena tend to be more sedate and exclusive than those in West Maui. Kihei has a few small hotels and several condominiums, making it ideal for family travel. The first resort on the island was at Hana, on the island's easternmost point. The Hana Maui still caters to the rich and famous on this remote, often wet, but incredibly beautiful side of the island.

A comprehensive, revealing look at how sugar came to be king in the Alexander and Baldwin Museum

ALEXANDER AND BALDWIN SUGAR MUSEUM

Central Maui is still sugar-cane country. Within minutes of leaving the airport, you're driving through cane fields. In the midst of these is a working sugar mill, Hawaii's largest, easily identified by three tall chimneys belching smoke. An old superintendent's house adjoining the mill has been converted into the island's only sugar museum. Although small, it has good exhibits documenting the history of Hawaii's sugar production, including its role in attracting immigrants who created the ethnic diversity of today. There are old artifacts, photographs and a working scale model of sugar mill machinery.
3957 Hansen Road, Puunene (off Route 350). Tel: (808) 871–8058. Open: Monday to Saturday 9:30am–4:30pm. Admission charge.

BAILEY HOUSE MUSEUM

Edward Bailey and his wife, Caroline, came to Maui in 1837 to teach at the Wailuku Female Seminary, which had been built six years earlier. When the seminary closed in 1849, the Baileys continued to live there with their five sons until 1882, when they moved to California.

Bailey was an accomplished painter and frequently returned to Hawaii to continue his work. A collection of his landscape paintings is displayed in the Bailey Gallery, which originally served as the seminary dining room and later as his studio. Other rooms display Hawaiian and missionary artifacts, which range from precontact *tapa* (tree-bark cloth) to Victorian office furniture. Outside is a canoe shed housing replicas of outrigger canoes and even Duke Kahanamoku's redwood surfboard. Adjoining the museum is an excellent shop offering a good selection of Hawaiiana and books at very reasonable prices.
2375-A Main Street, Wailuku. Tel: (808) 244–3326. Open: Monday to Friday 10am–4:30pm. Admission charge.

BALDWIN HOUSE

The Baldwin House is the oldest standing building in Lahaina and one of the most interesting historical sites on Maui (see page 92). It is one of the few fully restored buildings on the island. Dwight Baldwin, the first doctor and dentist in Hawaii, lived here with his wife and eight children. The house was built in the early 1830s from lava blocks cemented with crushed coral mortar, forming two-foot-thick walls which were then plastered over. Many of the furnishings are authentic and include the Baldwins' Steinway piano dating from 1859.

Front Street (opposite Pioneer Inn), Lahaina. Tel: (808) 661–3262. Open: daily 9am–4pm. Admission charge.

BANYAN TREE

You can't miss this vast tree – it covers a whole block in the heart of old Lahaina (see page 93). It was brought from India in 1873 as an 8-foot sapling and planted to commemorate the 50th anniversary of the Congregationalist Mission. Fifty years later over 500 people congregated under the tree for the centennial celebrations. Today, it spreads over almost an entire acre, rising 50 feet in the air.

CARTHAGINIAN II

See page 93.

HALE PA'I

Lahainaluna Road passes the Pioneer Sugar Mill and rises steeply up to Lahainaluna High School. Dating from 1831, it was the first American school to be established west of the Rocky Mountains. Hale Pa'i is the only original building still standing. In 1834 it saw the production of Hawaii's first newspaper, printed on a printing press brought round Cape Horn. The Hale now houses a

small printing museum and the archives of the Lahaina Restoration Foundation. The parking lot gives sweeping views over the whole of Lahaina and out to the little island of Lanai.

End of Lahainaluna Road, Lahaina. Tel: (808) 667–7074. Open: Monday to Thursday 10am–3pm. Free.

Above: the irresistible Banyan Tree
Below: printing the Bible was Hale Pa'i's first aim

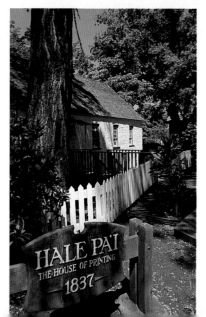

Sugar-cane was being grown in Hawaii even before Captain Cook first visited the Islands in 1778. Commercial growing started in the early 19th century, but it was the California Gold Rush in the mid-1800s that created the demand which established the industry. Immigrant workers brought into Hawaii from the Far East formed the basis of the diverse ethnic mix that exists today.

Water has always been critical to the success of sugar-cane plantations – it takes 250 gallons to produce a single pound of sugar. A Californian, Charles Sprekels, revolutionized the industry by building irrigation ditches across land that had

PLANTATIONS

previously been barren. By the end of the 18th century, growers were tapping underground water supplies and sugar was the Islands' primary cash crop. Today over 9 million tons of sugar-cane are produced annually. Although its economic importance is not what it used to be, the crop is still highly profitable.

Pineapples were introduced to Hawaii at about the same time commercial sugar-cane plantations were first established. It was not until the turn of the century, when Jim Dole decided that America was ready for pineapples, that the industry really took off. Dole canned

the fruit and shipped it to the mainland, and within a few years Hawaii was the biggest producer of pineapples in the world. In 1922 Dole bought the island of Lanai and turned it into the world's largest pineapple plantation.

From this high point the industry has slowly diminished. Nowadays, competition from the Far East, particularly the Philippines, has virtually destroyed the industry. Added to this, much agricultural land has been taken out of production to create even more golf courses for tourists.

Plantations are still to be found in central Oahu (see Dole Pineapple Pavilion and Del Monte Variety Garden), on Maui and, of course, Lanai, but even here, only a few acres remain under cultivation.

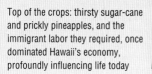

Top of the crops: thirsty sugar-cane and prickly pineapples, and the immigrant labor they required, once dominated Hawaii's economy, profoundly influencing life today

of the great experiences of Hawaii, and several companies offer trips both hiking and cycling on Haleakala. To get the best weather with clear conditions means reaching the crater rim by sunrise, but it is more than worth it. The rim is a 90-minute drive from Kahului, and most days the clouds start to roll in about mid-morning. The summit itself often remains clear, but the views disappear under a layer of cloud. The National Park provides daily weather information (tel: 808 572–7749). Early morning can be very cold at the summit, so take plenty of warm clothing.

The whole area, covering 27,284 acres, was designated a national park in 1961. Apart from the austere volcanic scenery, the crater is the only place where silverswords grow. These beautiful silver-grey plants – a protected endangered species – grow up to 8 feet in height, live for up to 20 years and end their lives sending up a stalk of hundreds of flowers. The best specimens can be seen on the Silversword Loop on the crater floor.

At park headquarters, approaching on Crater Road, you can get information, maps and camping permits. Just beyond is a trail-head parking lot on the left. The trail leads to two overlooks, Leleiwi and Kalahaku, with views of the crater.

At the end of the road is the Visitor Center, with good displays explaining the geology of Haleakala and ranger talks every hour. Maps and brochures are also available here.

Highway 37 to 377 to 378 to Haleakala. Tel: (808) 572–9306. Park open: 24 hours. Headquarters open: daily 7:30am–4pm. Visitor Center open: sunrise–3pm. Admission charge.

HALE PA'AHAO

On the corner of Waine'e and Prison streets stands a high wall constructed of stones taken from the Old Fort on Front Street. The wall was built during the 1850s by prisoners for their own personal use – as a prison. Hale Pa'ahao means "the stuck-in-irons house," referring to the wall shackles and ball-and-chain restraints. Most of the prisoners served time for deserting ship, drunkenness, working on the Sabbath or dangerous horseback riding. Today it holds only memories. The open courtyard provides a peaceful retreat from the frenzy of downtown Lahaina (see page 93).

Junction of Prison and Waine'e streets. Always open.

HALEAKALA

Haleakala is the biggest dormant volcano in the world. Its crater is 21 miles in circumference, 3,000 feet deep and contains over 30 miles of trails around nine cinder cones. Hiking in this moon-like environment, 10,000 feet high, is one

Moonscape to moonscape: Science City observatories on Haleakala's rim offer crystal-clear skies

HANA

Hana is more a state of mind than a destination. The town itself has very little to offer tourists, but the journey to it more than compensates for the lack of conventional attractions. This is one of Hawaii's most stunning coastlines, and peaceful, unspoilt Hana sits at the apex of the experience. Accommodations are sparse, apart from the Hotel Hana-Maui – one of the outstanding resort hotels of the world. There are only a couple of restaurants, and night life is nonexistent. The grandly named Hana Cultural Center, a one-room building, houses a motley collection of artifacts and photographs of old Hana. Adjacent is the old courthouse.

One of the more interesting sights is Hasegawa General Store, a classic old-time, family-run general store which sells everything from televisions to fishing supplies and food. If Harry Hasegawa doesn't stock it, you don't need it. *Hana Cultural Center, Uakea Road.*

Tel: (808) 248–8622. Open: daily 10am–4pm. Donation appreciated. Hasegawa General Store, 5165 Hana Highway. Tel: (808) 248–8231. Open: Monday to Saturday 8am–5:30pm, Sunday 9am–3:30pm.

Hana Cultural Center, Hana

HIGHWAY 340

One of the most dramatic stretches of road on Maui clings to the north coast of West Maui. It goes from Waihee near Wailuku all the way round to Kapalua, passing red sandstone cliffs, pounding surf and remote villages tucked away in sheltered bays. The middle section of the road is intended for the use of residents only, but no one enforces this policy. Highway 340 is paved for its whole length and can easily be negotiated in an ordinary car. The basic drive takes about two hours; allow extra time for stops. It is very winding and extremely narrow in places, but the stunning scenery of windward Maui is ample reward.

HUI NO'EAU VISUAL ARTS CENTER

Rotating exhibits of visual artists working on Maui are the main focus at the Center, housed in the 1917 Baldwin Mansion just outside Makawao in up-country Maui. There is also a small shop selling works by the artists and regular workshops in printing, drawing, printmaking, pottery and sculpture. The house is set in delightful grounds, and even though the weather on this side of the island tends toward the wet, the Center provides the perfect atmosphere for a creative getaway.

2841 Baldwin Avenue, Makawao. Tel: (808) 572–6560. Open: Tuesday to Sunday 10am–4pm. Admission charge.

IAO NEEDLE AND IAO VALLEY STATE PARK

The old town of Wailuku is now the county seat. The Iao Valley Road leads steeply out of town up into the green, and frequently misty, West Maui Mountains. The road ends in a big parking lot, where a short, steep path continues to a lookout point for the Iao Needle, whose reputation far exceeds its physical appearance. The valley has always been a place of pilgrimage for the Hawaiians, and the Needle was at one time used as a natural altar. It is actually a 1,200-foot-high basalt core from around which all the softer rocks have eroded, leaving the Needle standing like a giant tooth at the head of the valley.

The Iao Valley was the site of a bloody battle in 1790, when King Kamehameha the Great conquered Maui. According to legend, the dead filled the Iao Stream until it ran red.

Legend tells how Iao's father captured her lover and turned him into Iao's Needle

Kaanapali: a blue sea, a balmy day, a pristine beach; and Whalers Village (right)

Today the valley is one of the greenest places on the island, with moss-covered rock walls rising steeply in every direction. A number of easy paths lead into the park, but be prepared – there's more rain than sun in this part of Maui. *End of the Iao Valley Road. Open: daily 7am–7:45pm May to September, 7am–6:45pm the rest of the year.*

KAANAPALI

To many visitors, Kaanapali is synonymous with Maui. No less than six major hotels line this sunny 3-mile stretch of white-sand beaches on West Maui. The resort was planned in the 1950s by the Amfac Corporation to rival Waikiki. It was Hawaii's first planned destination resort and, with 600 acres, it is still the biggest.

The first hotel here was built round the Black Rock from which Kahekili, the last chief of Maui, would jump into the ocean to demonstrate his bravery. This

site was particularly significant, as Black Rock was considered the place where the souls of the dead leapt into their ancestral spirit land, and only people of great spiritual strength could compete with these souls and escape unharmed. The rock now serves as the stage for a nightly cliff demonstration at the Sheraton Maui.

The Whalers Village, an upscale shopping complex, has an excellent free Whaling Museum (open as store hours).

KEPANIWAI PARK AND HERITAGE GARDENS

One of the most interesting picnic spots on the island can be found just before the Iao Valley Road head. Kepaniwai Park was developed as a tribute to all the ethnic groups that make up Hawaii, with pavilions and gardens representing the Hawaiians, Chinese, Portuguese, Filipinos and Japanese. Each section contains examples of traditional architecture, and similarly the gardens reflect the various traditions. There are picnic tables throughout and entrance is free. The only problem is teenagers who congregate in the parking lots for illicit smoking and drinking, with music blaring out of boom boxes.

Off Iao Valley Road, west of Kalahui. Tel: (808) 243–7408. Open: daily. Free.

LAHAINA JODO MISSION

The original wooden temple on this Puunoa Point site burned down in 1968, and in the same year the Great Buddha and Temple Bell were completed, for the Centennial Celebration commemorating the arrival of Hawaii's first Japanese immigrants. The present temple, dating from 1970, is true to the traditions of old Japan, but the Buddha is what most people go to see. The largest of its kind outside Japan, the Great Buddha sits serenely against a backdrop of the West Maui Mountains. Cast in Kyoto from copper and bronze, it weighs 3½ tons.

12 Ala Moana Street, Lahaina. Open: daily. Free (donation box at door).

Steaming along: an all-too-brief rail journey links the resorts of Lahaina and Kaanapali

LAHAINA-KAANAPALI AND PACIFIC RAILROAD

The Sugarcane Train, as the railroad is more popularly called, chugs along on the slopes of the West Maui Mountains between Lahaina and Kaanapali. The trip is pure nostalgia, with a genuine old narrow-gauge steam engine belching out smoke on the 25-minute, 6-mile trip through fields of sugar-cane. Warm West Maui winds blow through the open passenger cars that have replaced the cane wagons originally pulled by the train.

Free transportation to the Lahaina station is provided from local hotels and from downtown Lahaina. The train is very popular, so advance booking is highly recommended.

Lahaina Station, Hinau Street. Tel: (808) 661–0089. Kaanapali Station, Highway 30, opposite Kekaa Drive exit. Puukoli Station, Puukoli Road. Six round-trips daily, 9am–5:30pm. Admission charge.

MAKAWAO

Up-country Maui has nothing in common with the beach resorts for which the island is best known. For a start, it rains a lot. The rest of the island can be bathed in sunshine, but rain will be falling on Makawao. This is cowboy country, and Makawao is a cowboy town. The false-front buildings lining the main street are straight out of the Wild West. Appropriately, every Fourth of July the biggest and best rodeo in the state is held here in the Oskie Rice Rodeo Arena. The town has lost none of its character and authenticity as a result of tourism.

MAUI TROPICAL PLANTATION

If you want to see all the crops of Hawaii growing in one place, then this is for you.

Maui Tropical Plantation features mangoes, macadamias and much more

A 40-minute narrated shuttle tour passes through 14 of Hawaii's best-known agricultural crops planted in the shape of a fan, whose spokes all point to the commercial heart of the operation–a Made-on-Maui Marketplace and a restaurant. Throughout the day there are demonstrations of *lei*-making and coconut-husking. Every Tuesday, Wednesday and Thursday evening there's a Hawaiian Country BBQ Party. As it says in the brochure: "a whole lot of Hawaiian hula-baloo and country carrying on."

Highway 30 and Waikapu. Tel: (808) 244–7643. Open: daily 9am–5pm; tours every 45 minutes starting at 9:15am and ending at 4pm. Barbecues from 4:45–7:30pm. Admission charge.

Actually numbering about two dozen, the so-called Seven Sacred Pools pour themselves into the sea

OHEO GULCH

The most famous site on the Hana Coast is Oheo Gulch, although few know it by that name. It is variously called either "The Seven Pools" or "The Seven Sacred Pools," much to the chagrin of the National Park Service. The nicknames, reputedly a promotional scheme by a local hotel, have had an unexpectedly successful effect. The pools are neither seven nor sacred. Some 24 of them cascade down the Kipahulu Valley in Haleakala National Park.

About 10 miles out of Hana, Route 31 crosses an arched cement bridge. From the bridge, to the left, the lower pools can be seen falling down to the sea. A little further on is a large parking lot, adjacent to the park headquarters. The lower pools are easily reached by a well-marked path leading from there. They can be crowded at peak times (although more people look than swim). It's more interesting to climb to the upper pools, across the bridge and up towards Waimoku Falls (ask at the ranger station for directions). Few people venture up here, and you could well have a swimming pool all to yourself.

SEAMEN'S HOSPITAL

During the whaling era, sailors were often abandoned in Lahaina to lighten the load. Many had diseases picked up on their travels, and spent their last days at the Seamen's Hospital. Half the Congressional budget for the care of all US seamen was going to this hospital until it was discovered that some of the "patients" were long since deceased. The building now houses commercial offices and is not open to the public, but the exterior can be viewed from the grounds. *Front and Baker Streets, Lahaina.*

SUNRISE PROTEA FARM

On the slopes of Haleakala, at 2,000 to 4,000 feet above sea level, conditions conspire to produce some of the finest protea flowers in the world. You can wander round the easy-to-find Sunrise Farm to see the plants growing, with their showy bracts and dense flower heads. A shop selling the proteas will ship them worldwide.

Box 416A, Haleakala Crater Road. Tel: (808) 878–2119. Open: daily 8am–4pm. Closed: Christmas Day.

Artistic arrangements at Sunrise Protea Farm

TEDESCHI VINEYARDS

High on the southern slopes of Haleakala, vineyards incongruously flow down the mountainside. Hawaii is certainly not known for its wine, and one taste will demonstrate why, but the Tedeschi Vineyards continue to attract enthusiastic crowds to their tasting room. The novelty value alone makes this an interesting attraction; add the beautiful surroundings of the Ulupalakua Ranch, and even "Pineapple Blanc" or "Maui Blush" takes on considerably more appeal. The winery is housed in the old ranch jailhouse, and free guided tours are offered daily. A few miles past the winery, the paved road ends and dirt begins, eventually joining the road to Hana.

Highway 37, 10 miles past the junction with Highway 377. Tel: (808) 878–6058. Open: daily 9am–5pm; tours 9:30am–2:30pm. Free.

WO HING TEMPLE

Right in the center of Lahaina's bustling tourist district, the Wo Hing Temple preserves a way of life going back to 1909 when the Chinese sugar-cane laborers formed the Wo Hing Society. In 1912 they built a fraternal hall and cookhouse equipped with traditional Chinese fire pits and utensils. The site is now a museum of early Chinese culture in Maui, and the cookhouse is used to show films on Hawaii made by Thomas Edison in 1898 and 1906.

858 Front Street, Lahaina. Tel: (808) 661–3262. Open: Monday to Saturday 9am–4:30pm, Sunday 11am–4:30pm. Donations accepted.

The lovingly restored Wo Hing Temple museum

Old Lahaina

This old Maui whaling town is a thriving tourist destination, second only to Waikiki in terms of vitality. The old part of town teems with historic sites, sitting amidst modern boutiques and cafés. This walk gives a basic introduction to many of the most significant sights. *Allow 1 hour.*

There is a parking lot off Dickenson Street just behind the Baldwin House. Walk down Dickenson Street to the corner.

1 THE MASTERS' READING ROOM

Together with the Baldwin House, this is one of the two oldest Western structures on Maui. The Lahaina Restoration Foundation is housed in this coral block building, and although the building is not open to the public, you can visit to pick up maps and brochures on Lahaina.

2 BALDWIN HOUSE

The is the showcase museum of the Lahaina Restoration Society. It is fully restored with period furniture, including a Steinway piano made in 1859 (see page 81).
Cross Front Street and walk directly towards the waterfront to a small park.

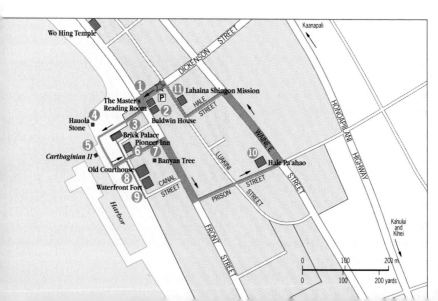

3 THE BRICK PALACE

Only the foundations remain of this palace, the first Western building in Hawaii. It was built for Kamehameha I by two British ex-convicts from Australia in 1800, but it is doubtful that he ever lived here. Until the 1850s, it was mainly used for storage.

4 HAUOLA STONE

Just over the sea wall next to the Brick Palace is a large chair-shaped rock, believed to have curative powers if you sit in it and let the sea wash over you.

5 CARTHAGINIAN II

It is impossible to miss this impressive schooner dominating Lahaina's seafront. This is a replica of an old square-rigged sailing ship built to replace *Carthaginian I*, which ran aground in 1972. The ship is a museum devoted to whales and whaling. Below decks there are displays of artifacts, videos and photographs.
Cross the road.

6 PIONEER INN

The Pioneer Inn, built in 1901, was the only accommodation in West Maui until the late 1950s.

7 THE BANYAN TREE

Next to the Pioneer Inn stands this famous tree, planted in 1873 and now covering almost an acre. It was planted to mark the 50th anniversary of the Protestant missionaries' arrival in Lahaina (see page 81).

8 OLD COURTHOUSE

The Banyan Tree has almost engulfed this building, constructed in 1859 from the remains of Kamehameha III's palace. Art galleries now occupy the Courthouse as well as the Old Jail in the basement.

Carthaginian II recalls the heyday of whaling

9 WATERFRONT FORT

In its heyday the Fort guarded Lahaina with 47 cannons, but its eventual destiny was to be torn down to build a jail. The ruins of the Fort are on either side of the Old Courthouse.
Turn right into Front Street and left into Prison Street. Walk two blocks to Waine'e Street.

10 HALE PA'AHAO

On the corner is the prison built by convicts from the stones of Waterfront Fort. It was Lahaina's prison from 1854 and its interior was very familiar to drunken sailors (see page 84).
Turn left into Waine'e Street, left into Hale Street and right into Luakini Street.

11 LAHAINA SHINGON MISSION

This plantation-era Buddhist temple is typical of temples erected all over Maui by immigrant Japanese laborers.
Continue along Luakini Street and turn left into Dickenson Street. The parking lot is immediately on the left.

Carthaginian II – tel: (808) 661–8527. Open: 9am–4:30pm. Admission charge.

The Hana Highway

The drive to Hana and beyond ranks as the finest drive in the Pacific. The road winds through moss-covered gorges, past cascading waterfalls, black-sand beaches and luxuriant rain forest. The area certainly merits more than a one-day visit – and if accommodation can be arranged, most of the worst traffic can be avoided. After Paia, there are no petrol stations or shops until Hana. *Allow a full day.*

1 PAIA

This is where the road really starts. Flower power is alive and well in this hangover from the 1960s. Wandering round the art galleries, craft shops and cafés you'll notice nostalgic, although not necessarily legal, aromas frequently drifting through the air.
Drive on to the 11-mile marker.

2 PUOHOKAMOA FALLS

The falls at this popular stop are a modest sample of the delights to come.
Drive on to the 16-mile marker.

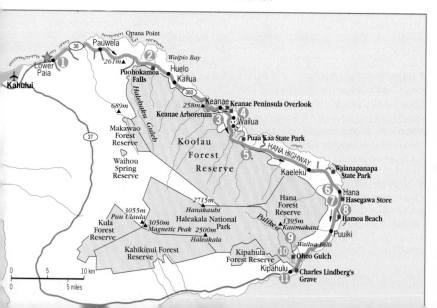

3 KEANAE ARBORETUM

This freely accessible park is divided into native forest, introduced forest and traditional Hawaiian plants and foodstuffs. All plants are clearly labeled along well-maintained trails.

4 KEANAE PENINSULA OVERLOOK

A few hundred yards past the Arboretum, a car park on the left offers sweeping views of the Keanae Peninsula with its taro patches, palms and banana trees.
Drive on to the 22-mile marker.

5 PUAA KAA STATE PARK

The toilet facilities are the most important reason for stopping at this otherwise uninteresting little park. A tiny waterfall spills into a pool that looks far from inviting.
Continue to Hana.

6 HANA

See page 85.

7 HASEGAWA STORE

Leaving Hana, you'll find Harry Hasegawa's famous store on the left. Harry stocks just about anything you could possibly need (see page 85).
Drive just over 1 mile south of Hana, then turn left and continue for another mile, down Haneoo Road to Hamoa Beach. Note that after Hana the highway has a new designation and the mileage markers descend in sequence. Also, the condition of the road deteriorates.

8 HAMOA BEACH

This is the beach James Michener once described as the best in the Pacific.
Continue to the 45-mile marker.

The proprietor himself, Harry Hasegawa

9 WAILUA FALLS

These are the most easily accessible, dramatic falls on this tour, only a couple of minutes' walk from the road.
Continue to the 42-mile marker.

10 OHEO GULCH

The so-called "Seven Sacred Pools" lie within Haleakala National Park (see page 90). In fact, the pools are not sacred (although it was *kapu* for menstruating women to bathe in them) and there are far more than seven. A series of waterfalls link the lower pools, which make perfect swimming holes (be careful of slippery rocks and submerged rocks and ledges). They are a 10-minute walk from the Visitor Center.
Continue to the 41-mile marker and turn left on an unpaved road just over a mile beyond Oheo Gulch.

11 CHARLES LINDBERGH'S GRAVE

Charles Lindbergh (1902–1974) was the pioneer pilot who made the first nonstop solo flight from New York to Paris in 1927. He built his cliff-side home in Kipahulu in 1968, and in this magnificent solitude the legendary aviator spent his last years in retirement. Look for Palapala Hoomau Congregational Church through the trees. Lindbergh's grave, with a volcanic stone platform, is well marked in the churchyard, which overlooks the ocean.
Return along the same route.

Hawaii

*H*awaii is commonly called the Big Island, and with good reason. Almost double the size of its closest rival, it continues to grow weekly as volcanic lava pours into the ocean, adding new land mass.

Mauna Loa, rising 13,677 feet (4,169m) above sea level, is the world's largest active volcano, last erupting in 1950. Mauna Kea, its dormant twin volcanic peak, rises to 13,796 feet (4,205m), making it the largest island-based mountain in the world. Just north of Mauna Kea is the 225,000-acre Parker Ranch, the biggest privately owned ranch in the USA.

Kilauea is less impressive in size, but more than makes up for it in volcanic activity. It is one of the world's most active volcanoes and in 1990 completely destroyed the town of Kalapana. Pele,

The Kohala Coast, Big Island

the goddess of fire, is taken very seriously in these parts!

After a day's skiing at the summit of Mauna Kea, you can wander through tropical rain forests looking for orchids. The Kohala Coast can be bathed in sunshine while rain pours down in Hilo. A land of sharper contrasts is hard to imagine.

It was on the Big Island that the first seafaring Polynesians stepped ashore, and centuries later it became the island of kings. Kamehameha I was born here on the North Kohala Coast, and his bones are still hidden somewhere on the island. Kamehameha III was born near Kailua-Kona. Some of the most

impressive *heiaus* (temples) are on the Big Island, and the one known as the 'Place of Refuge' is among the best-preserved historic sites in Polynesia.

Travel time between sites is much greater than on the neighboring islands. Try to resist the temptation to see too much, or what you'll see most of is the inside of a car!

Celebrate sunset over a lingering cocktail

HAWAII

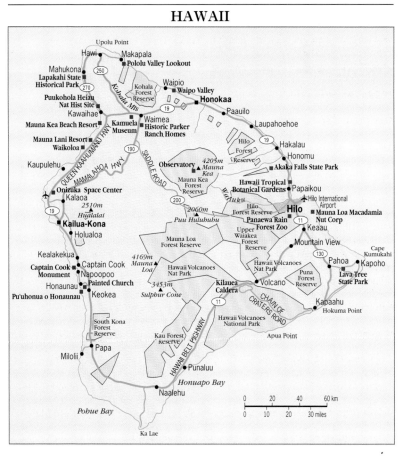

At Hikiau Heiau Captain Cook was ritually recognized as the reincarnated god Lono

AKAKA FALLS STATE PARK

The falls are a 10-minute drive through sugar-cane plantations. The journey will take longer if you stop at the quaint old plantation town of Honomu. There's not much here now other than a row of false-front buildings that evoke another era.

Akaka Falls are among the most easily accessible tropical wilderness experiences on the Big Island. From the trail-head parking lot, follow a paved loop trail through exotic rain forest. The trail is surrounded by bamboo groves, orchids, azaleas, giant philodendrons and a multitude of other flora that grow to gargantuan sizes.

The 400-foot Kahuna Falls can be seen from an overlook before the trail enters a tunnel of vegetation. Within a few minutes Akaka Falls can be seen plunging 420 feet through the air in a sheer drop.
Route 220 off Highway 19.

AMY GREENWELL ETHNOBOTANICAL GARDEN

Covering over 10 acres of land, this rather esoteric garden is an outpost of Honolulu's Bishop Museum. This is not a garden of beautiful blooms and carefully tended flower beds. At first glance it appears to be just a more organized extension of the surrounding countryside, and that's exactly what it is. The garden is divided into six vegetation zones and focuses on the themes of traditional Hawaiian land and plant use.

When the garden is finally completed, there will be hundreds of wild and domesticated plants that have been essential to the cultural and economic lives of native Hawaiians. This is a research and educational center preserving Hawaiian traditions, not a tourist attraction, but self-guided tours are available on weekday mornings.
Highway 11, Captain Cook. Tel: (808) 323–3318. Open: Monday to Friday 9am–noon. Guided tours 2nd Saturday of every month at 10am. Free.

CAPTAIN COOK MONUMENT

Kealakekua Bay is reached by a steep road dropping down from Highway 11 through coffee and macadamia nut plantations. At the end of the road, turn right to a small parking lot by a simple pier. A lone white obelisk is visible in the distance across Kealakekua Bay. It was on that spot, in 1779, that the English explorer Captain James Cook was killed, and possibly eaten, by the native villagers who had originally considered him a god.

By the side of the parking lot is Hikiau Heiau. This ancient Hawaiian temple was the site of the first Christian ceremony to be performed in the Islands, a burial service conducted by Captain Cook for one of his crewmen (see pages 100–1).

Precontact civilization on Hawaii depended on the plants at the Amy Greenwell Garden

CHAIN OF CRATERS ROAD

Chain of Craters Road starts from Crater Rim Drive in Hawaii Volcanoes National Park. The 4,000-foot drop to sea level takes about 30 minutes and passes through volcanic desolation, skirting craters and lava flows as it dips towards the sea.

At one time it was possible to drive from Puna all the way to Volcanoes National Park, but a massive lava flow, several miles wide, severed the road. In 1989 another lava flow destroyed the Wahaula Visitor Center at the bottom of the road. Rangers lead walks onto the still-hot lava flow from here, and at night you can see the red glow of magma coursing through lava tubes just beneath the surface. Hiking onto the flow should be undertaken with the greatest caution and only under the supervision of a park ranger. The Volcanic Update is a 24-hour recorded information service on the latest eruptions (tel: 808 967–7977).

How the Earth was formed: a process still under way along Chain of Craters Road

CAPTAIN COOK

Captain James Cook was on his third voyage to the Pacific looking for the Northwest Passage when he made his fateful discovery of Hawaii in 1778. On January 18th, his ship HMS *Resolution* and its companion, HMS *Discovery*, sighted the island of Oahu. On January 20th they landed at Waimea on Kauai. Here they traded brass medallions and iron nails for fish, pork and yams.

The sailors were impressed with the "friendliness" of the native women – apparently a test to see if these strangers were divine or merely mortal with the usual appetites. The sailors left no doubt about that (and passed on venereal diseases at the same time).

Cook named his discovery the Sandwich Islands after his patron, the Earl of Sandwich, First Lord of the Admiralty. His expedition continued on to Alaska, and it was almost a year before Cook returned to the Islands. He spent eight weeks unsuccessfully looking for a harbor on Maui. During this time the coastline of the island was mapped by Lt. William Bligh, later to captain the *Bounty*.

The ships then sailed to the island of Hawaii, where a bizarre and fatal series of coincidences occurred. On January 16, 1779, Cook sailed into Kealakekua Bay during a celebration for the god Lono, who, according to legend, would one day return to Earth. Kealakekua Bay was considered to be Lono's sacred harbor, and the god was always depicted as a small figure on top of a tall, mast-like pole, with sail-like sheets of *tapa* cloth hanging down. Cook's arrival seemed the fulfillment of the prophecy. He and his crew members were led to a temple, where they were treated like deities.

After a few weeks, however, one of the sailors died. This convinced the Hawaiians that the white men were ordinary mortals after all,

The death of Captain Cook, February 14, 1779

and relations quickly soured. The theft of a longboat from the *Discovery* became the pivotal event in the breakdown. Cook wanted to take King Kalaniopuu on board ship as a hostage until the longboat was returned. This miscalculated strategy led to the uprising that cost Cook his life at the age of 51 and ended the greatest era of Pacific exploration.

Cultivated jungle meets untamed sea at the matchless Hawaii Tropical Botanical Gardens

HAWAII TROPICAL BOTANICAL GARDENS

Clinging to the shore of Onomea Bay, one of the Big Island's most beautiful bays, these gardens extend along four miles of scenic drive north of Hilo. If time is limited, the gardens can be glimpsed from stops along the drive, but this is no substitute for spending time on a self-guided tour. Access is by private shuttle, and no cars are allowed down.

Over 1,800 species of plants from many parts of the world thrive here, and resident flamingos and macaws enhance the exotic atmosphere. All the plants are labeled with both English and Latin names, together with country of origin. This coast of the Big Island is extremely wet, which of course helps the gardens but dampens the spirits of visitors. If it happens to be raining, which is highly probable, umbrellas are available for loan, free of charge.

PO Box 1415, Hilo. Tel: (808) 964–5233. Open: daily 8:30am–4:30pm. Shuttle leaves every 20 minutes, from 8:50am. Closed: Thanksgiving, Christmas, New Year's. Admission charge.

HAWAII VOLCANOES NATIONAL PARK

Of all the sights of Hawaii, this has to be the most awesome – a chance to encounter an active volcano and experience the tremendous forces that formed the land. The park was established in 1916 and covers 377 square miles, from the 4,169m (13,677-foot) summit of Mauna Loa to the ocean. Trails of every standard weave throughout the park, but the center of activities is around Kilauea, the volcano that keeps on erupting. Since 1983 lava flows have destroyed 178 homes and added over 200 acres to the island.

Kilauea Visitor Center and park headquarters lie just off the Hawaii Belt Highway past the entrance station. This is the obvious place to start a visit; maps and guides are available here, together with up-to-the-minute information on volcanic activity. Crater Rim Drive circles Kilauea's caldera and craters, passing through rain forest and desert, and gives access to several scenic stops and short walks. Highlights include Sulphur Banks, Halema'uma'u Crater, Steam Vents and Devastation Trail (all clearly marked on the free map given at the entrance station).

Start the drive in an anticlockwise direction, stopping at the Jaggar Museum for invaluable background information in the form of photographs, models and videos. (See also Chain of Craters Road on page 99, Thurston Lava Tube on page 116, and pages 118–19.)

Off Highway 11. Tel: (808) 967–7311. Visitor Center and Jagger Museum open: daily 8am–5pm. Admission charge for park; museum free.

Keep a respectful distance from volcanic steam vents and sizzling "skylights"

HILO

Although the population is under 38,000, Hilo is the second biggest city in the state. It is also one of the oldest permanently settled towns. Hilo's annual rainfall of 133 inches keeps tourists away, prices low and the town as quiet and unspoilt as any in the Islands. Winter sees the heaviest rains, but even then the clouds let loose predictably in the afternoon. The benefit of all this rain is seen in the profusion of greenery and flowers. Gardens abound, even at the airport, where 20 acres of exotic flowers line the runways.

Old Hilo is a classic tropical town straight out of a Somerset Maugham novel. Weather-worn, tin-roofed buildings line the streets as they do in sleepy little ports throughout the South Pacific. Ignore the rain and enjoy the ambience (see page 122).

HISTORIC PARKER RANCH HOMES

Waimea virtually owes its existence to the Parker family, so it's appropriate that the Parker Ranch Homes should be among the premier visitor attractions. A grand eucalyptus-lined drive leads to a parking lot, a small cabin and an ordinary-looking ranch-style house – the mansion suggested by that driveway doesn't materialize! Puuopelu, the larger of the two homes, is deceptive, however. It was built in 1852 by John Palmer Parker II, and in 1943 Parker's heir, Richard Smart, inherited the ranchlands and the house. Smart was an avid collector of paintings, and in 1969, to accommodate his treasures, he gutted the house in order to raise the ceiling to 19 feet. Today the front door opens to reveal an elegant salon.

Smart may have been one of America's biggest ranchers, but his heart was in the theatre and he became a well-known actor of his day with a taste for elegance. In art he liked Impressionism, and his collection still hangs on the walls of Puuopelu and provides the main attraction for visitors. There are over a hundred works, including paintings by Renoir, Degas, Vlaminck and even Chagall. For a private collection, particularly on a Hawaiian ranch, it is quite remarkable.

The cabin next to Puuopelu is the reconstructed Mana Home, the original Parker Ranch homestead that was built in 1847 by John Palmer Parker. The simple home has been authentically furnished to re-create the living conditions of the day.

Highway 190, ¼ mile south of Waimea. Tel: (808) 885-7655. Open: daily 10am–5pm. Closed: major holidays. Admission charge.

Outwardly modest, this Parker Ranch house contains a superb private art collection

HULIHE'E PALACE

John Adams Kuakini, brother-in-law of King Kamehameha III, was governor of the Big Island when he built the Hulihe'e Palace in 1838. The Victorian coral and lava palace was subsequently used by the royal family as a summer retreat until 1916. It is now a museum run by the Daughters of Hawaii. Prince Kuhio auctioned off all the furniture from the palace, but each piece was numbered and the name of the buyer

Posing for this role reversal looks uncomfortable, not to mention impossible!

recorded. The Daughters of Hawaii have painstakingly tracked down most of the furniture and persuaded the owners to relinquish it for the cause. The interior is now furnished authentically with original pieces, including Queen Kapiolani's four-poster bed and a massive dining table, 70 inches in diameter, made from a single koa log (see pages 124–5).
75–5718 Ali'i Drive, Kailua-Kona. Tel: (808) 329–1877. Open: daily 9am–4pm. Admission charge.

KAILUA PIER

Built in 1915, this pier is the main center of activity in Kailua-Kona, and is a mecca for Pacific blue marlin fishermen. During the season these huge fish are hauled out of the water and weighed on the pier's scales (some have weighed in at over 1,000 pounds). As well as fishing boats coming and going all day long, Atlantic Submarines (see page 136) and Nautilus Semi-Submersible both use Kailua Pier as a launch area (see pages 124–5).

This is also a good spot from which to view the end of the grueling Ironman Triathlon. Every October more than a thousand entrants attempt to swim 2.4 miles in rough ocean, cycle for 112 miles, then end with a 26.2 mile run, whose finish line is in Kailua Bay just by the pier.

KAMUELA MUSEUM

This is the biggest privately owned museum in the state, and certainly the most eccentric. It houses the 50-year collection of Albert K Solomon and his wife, Harriet, who claims to be the great-granddaughter of the founder of Parker Ranch. The collection covers just about everything, from stuffed lizards to a Ford Model-T tire remover, displayed in no particular order. The handwritten descriptions are about the only element that differentiates this place from a junk shop.

Junction of Highways 19 and 250, Waimea. Tel: (808) 885–4724. Open: daily 8am–5pm. Admission charge.

Time-worn structures at Lapakahi Park need careful visitors to survive 600 more years

KOHALA COAST

This barren strip on the Big Island's west coast has the lowest rainfall in the state. It is not uncommon to fly out of Honolulu in torrential rain and arrive 30 minutes later in Kona in brilliant sunshine. This favorable climate has resulted in the proliferation of several luxury resorts, including some of the world's finest.

From Kona Airport the coast is a 30-minute drive north on Route 11. The road passes through desolate, chaotic lava fields that look like recently bulldozed earth. The lava is peppered with white coral graffiti, practically a folk art form in its own right.

The three big resorts – Waikoloa, Mauna Lani Resort and Mauna Kea Beach Resort – are like oases in this lava desert. Each has at least one championship golf course. An ancient trail follows the coastline, and a remarkable number of historic sites punctuate the resort development (see page 120).

LAPAKAHI STATE HISTORICAL PARK

Six hundred years ago there was a thriving fishing village here on the north Kohala Coast. It is easy to understand why the ancient Hawaiians were drawn to this glorious location overlooking clear blue waters. Excavations reveal the old stone house foundations, and some of the dwellings have been reconstructed. A self-guided tour round the park takes at least one hour.

Off Highway 270, Mahukona. Tel: (808) 889–5566. Open: daily 8am–4pm. Free.

LAVA TREE STATE PARK

Over 200 years ago molten lava from Kilauea engulfed a grove of ohia trees. The lava solidified round the moisture-

A "lava tree" testifies to old volcanic flow

LYMAN MUSEUM AND MISSION HOUSE

The Lyman Museum is one of Hilo's few tourist attractions. It may not be on a par with Honolulu's museums, but at least the exhibits can be seen in a brief visit. The mineral collection is particularly fine, and there is a good collection of seashells. The ground-floor Island Heritage Gallery is devoted to culture and anthropology.

The old New England-style frame house, next to the modern museum building, was built by the Lymans themselves in 1839. They lived there as missionaries with their eight children and frequently entertained guests, including Mark Twain and Robert Louis Stevenson. The house has been beautifully restored with many of the Lymans' own furnishings, including a working melodeon, antique china and handmade furniture. Visits to the Mission House are by tour only, which begin on the half hour during the morning and on the hour during the afternoon.

rich trunks to form a shell, while the oncoming lava flowed down into cracks that had opened up in the ground. The black lava "stumps" left behind look like grotesque garden ornaments in what is now a verdant tropical park. A short loop trail takes about 30 minutes to complete. *Take Highway 130 out of Keaau. Just past Pahoa, turn left on Highway 132. The park is 2 miles down on the left. Open: daily. Free.*

276 Haili Street, Hilo. Tel: (808) 935–5021. Open: Monday to Saturday 9am–5pm, Sunday 1–4pm. Admission charge.

Mauna Kea Beach on the sunny Kohala Coast

MACADAMIA NUTS

Rich volcanic soil, tropical sun and abundant rain make ideal conditions for growing macadamia nuts. Hawaii's first seedlings were brought over from Australia and the tree was grown

mainly for ornamental purposes, as the nut's hard shell was thought too difficult to crack. Happily, that problem was got round, and the nuts – about the size and shape of hazelnuts, but much richer and tastier – are now a mainstay of the state's agriculture. The trees mature slowly, but the grower's patience is rewarded with decades of fruit bearing.

The world's largest grower is the Mauna Loa Macadamia Nut Company, with an orchard of over a million trees. The road to their visitor center and factory passes 3 miles of macadamia orchards. The visitor center is little more than a glorified shop, but the adjacent factory is open (weekdays only) for tours which show the nuts being processed – everything from roasting to coating with chocolate. Note that the end products can cost less in town than at the visitor center shop.

In complete contrast, an authentic old-fashioned operation can be found at the Kona Coast Macadamia Nut and Candy Factory. Although it's no match in size or sophistication compared to Mauna Loa, it gives a much more down-to-earth view of nut-processing in unpretentious surroundings. Refreshingly, the small retail area seems almost an afterthought.

Kona Coast Macadamia Nut and Candy

Factory, junction Highway 11 and Middle Keei Road, Honaunau. Tel: (808) 328–8141. Open: Monday to Saturday 9am–4:30pm. Free. Mauna Loa Macadamia Nut Visitor Center, end of Macadamia Road off Highway 11, 5 miles south of Hilo. Tel: (808) 966–9301. Open: daily 8:30am–5pm (factory Monday to Friday only). Free.

MAUNA KEA

At almost 14,000 feet (4,205m) high, dormant Mauna Kea dominates the Big Island. Snow is a permanent feature here (its name means "White Mountain"), and during the winter there is even skiing. The amazing complex of astronomical

The lower slopes of the sleeping Mauna Kea volcano, dotted with strangely hued rocks

The gently rolling, formally arranged Nani Mau Gardens feature an area of orchids

observatories at the summit are considered the best in the world because of the crystal-clear air, the lack of light pollution, and its altitude, which places it above 40 percent of the Earth's atmosphere. Astronomers from around the world book telescope time months in advance; visitors can look at the telescopes, if not through them, with much greater ease. A four-wheel drive vehicle is needed to get to the summit, and tours are available.

Waipio Valley Shuttle and Tours, end of Route 240, Waipio. Tel: (808) 775–7121.

MOKUAIKAUA CHURCH

This is the oldest Christian church in Hawaii, built by Protestant missionaries in 1836 (see page 125). The 112-foot steeple, with chimes that sound hourly, is still the tallest structure in town. The church was built from lava stones using a mortar of crushed coral. Inside there are a few exhibits, including a Polynesian navigational chart and a model of the

brig *Thaddeus*, which brought the missionaries.

Off Ali'i Drive, opposite Hulihe'e Palace, Kailua-Kona. Open: daily 6am–6pm.

NANI MAU GARDENS

There is no shortage of gardens on the verdant northeast coast of Hawaii, and Nani Mau is one of the biggest of its type. The 53 acres of carefully landscaped gardens are a floral theme park, with waterways, a lily pond, great displays of anthurium and heliconias, orchids and hibiscus, plus an extensive annual garden. Altogether there are over 2,000 plant varieties. The well-maintained paths are very easy to walk round, but golf carts are available if necessary. There is also a narrated shuttle tour available. This side of the island is wet, and umbrellas are thoughtfully provided.

421 Makalika Road, Hilo. Tel: (808) 959–3541. Open: daily 8am–5pm. Admission charge.

ONIZUKA SPACE CENTER

The Space Center is an educational facility dedicated to the memory of Hawaii's first astronaut, Ellison Onizuka, who was tragically killed along with six other crew members when the space shuttle *Challenger* exploded during its launch in 1986. In addition to the inevitable space suit and moon rock displays, there are several interactive exhibits. At the Manned Maneuvering Unit replica, you can test your skills with the hand controls to rendezvous with an object in space. Another exhibit lets you launch a miniature space shuttle, and there are several audiovisual computer exhibits. The Space Theater shows various aspects of space travel through the day.

The center is located at Keahole Airport, just north of Kailua-Kona, directly across from the car rental counters. It provides a useful diversion for children when the lines are impossibly long or flights delayed. *PO Box 833, Kailua-Kona. Tel: (808) 329–3441. Open: daily 8:30am–4:30pm. Closed: Thanksgiving, Christmas and New Year's Day. Admission charge.*

Amazing murals deceive the eye within the wooden walls of the Painted Church

THE PAINTED CHURCH

St Benedict's is a very short detour from the road to Pu'uhonua o Honaunau, and well worth the visit. Father Everest Gielen, a Belgian priest, built the church in 1928 and decided to improve the simple wooden building by painting the ceiling in the tradition of Michelangelo and adding murals depicting religious scenes. He also painted a vaulted nave to give the effect of a grand European cathedral. Father Everest, who did most of the work at night by oil lamp, was transferred off the island before he could complete his masterpiece. The lower panels of the church were finally completed in 1964 by George Heidler from Georgia. This is a wonderful example of genuine folk art. A statue of Father Damien, who built a church 2 miles from here in 1864, sits outside the church.

PANAEWA RAIN FOREST ZOO

The 12-acre Panaewa Rain Forest Zoo, just outside Hilo, is the only zoo in America to be set in a natural rain forest – the Panaewa Forest Reserve – which gets 125 inches of rain annually. It's a

A stunning vista overlooking the forbidding northern cliffs, past Pololu Valley

modest enterprise with a very limited range of animals, and may not be worth visiting if time is short.

Off Highway 11, 1 mile down Mamaki Street, Hilo. Tel: (808) 959–7224. Open: daily 9am–4pm. Closed: Christmas and New Year's Day. Free.

PARKER RANCH VISITOR CENTER AND MUSEUM

John Palmer Parker, in 1809, agreed to round up the island's feral sheep, goats and cattle in exchange for a homestead. From these humble beginnings the homestead has grown to what is reckoned to be America's biggest private ranch, at over 224,000 acres. The visitor center, tucked away at the back of the Parker Ranch Shopping Center, is comprised of a cinema, small museum and store – with a big emphasis on the store. A 20-minute film presents the history and day-to-day operation of the ranch. The museum is a small, static collection of artifacts from over 140 years of ranching. Inevitably the tour ends in the store, where you can buy almost anything with a Parker Ranch logo splashed across it.

Parker Ranch Shopping Center, Waimea. Tel: (808) 885–7655. Open: daily 9am–5pm. Admission charge.

POLOLU VALLEY LOOKOUT

Highway 270 comes to an abrupt end after Makapala. Ahead are precipitous cliffs and deep valleys barring the way to Waipio Valley. There are sweeping views of a classic taro farming valley, and a switchback trail leads down through a tunnel of shrubs to a beautiful black-sand beach.

Highway 270, Makapala.

PUAKO PETROGLYPH ARCHEOLOGICAL PRESERVE

See page 120.

PU'UHONUA O HONAUNAU

Historic sites throughout Polynesia usually consist of little more than a pile of rocks. This one is an exception.

The ancient Hawaiians believed that if sacred laws (*kapu*) were broken, the only escape was to the closest place of refuge (*pu'uhonua*), where a priest could absolve the offender. Pu'uhonua o Honaunau, also known as the City of Refuge, was the biggest of these sanctuaries, built over a 20-acre lava peninsula on the Kona Coast. The site is now part of a 180-acre national historic park.

The Great Wall dominates the site. This lava rock barricade, built without mortar, is 10 feet high, 17 feet wide and 1,000 feet long. Inside there are three *heiaus* (temples) – the sanctuary which escaping *kapu*-breakers had to reach. Besides the main structure, there are examples of traditional houses and ancient arts and crafts. All the structures on the site have been faithfully reconstructed following old drawings by early sailors, and they now comprise the most authentic and complete site of its kind in the state. Self-guided tour maps are available at park headquarters.

Off Highway 160, 4 miles south of Kealakekua Bay. Tel: (808) 328–2326. Open: daily 7:30am–5:30pm. Admission charge.

A grimacing wooden statue, Pu'uhonua o Honaunau

PUUKOHOLA HEIAU NATIONAL HISTORIC SITE

Kamehameha, not yet king, built this tiered *heiau* in 1791 after a prophecy that it would ensure victory over rival islands. The *heiau* is still considered sacred by native Hawaiians, and no one is allowed onto it. The geography of the site makes it almost impossible to view the *heiau* as little more than a heap of volcanic rocks. However, a small visitor center has interpretative literature, models and a video explaining the history and significance of the site.

Off Highway 270, near Kawaihae. Tel: (808) 882–7218. Open: daily 7:30am–4pm. Free.

ROYAL KONA COFFEE MILL AND MUSEUM

Although the Hawaiian Visitors Bureau's warrior sign for this attraction is posted on Highway 11, the mill and museum are actually situated almost at the bottom of the road to Kealakekua Bay near Napoopoo. Although the mill is not open to the public, there is a shop masquerading as a museum where, in addition to T-shirts, chocolate-covered macadamia nuts and packets of coffee, you can view coffee being roasted and see a collection of old coffee plantation machinery. An exhibit of badly sun-faded photographs depicts the process and history of coffee production; on a more positive note, samples of different coffees are available for free tasting.

Napoopoo Road, between Captain Cook

The sacred remains of Puukohola Heiau; below, cooled wrinkles of lava beside Saddle Road

and Napoopoo. Tel: (808) 328 2511.
Open: daily 9am–5pm. Free.

SADDLE ROAD

The middle of the Big Island is crossed
by this high, desolate road. Most car
rental companies prohibit driving on it,
which makes Saddle Road an irresistible
adventure to some people. What the car
companies have against the road is hard
to understand. The road is well-surfaced,
as wide as most roads on the island, and
no more remote than many other areas.
It is certainly remote, however, and there
are no facilities at all along the way.
Rental companies don't police the road,
and many people risk the drive without
any problems. But if you do break down,
you may have a lot of explaining to do –
never mind the expense of rescue.

Saddle Road traverses some of the
best scenery on the island, across old lava
fields from the eruptions of Mauna Loa,
past caves and even a nene sanctuary
(the nene is the state bird). This is also
the road by which to reach the Mauna
Kea Observatories (see page 108).

COFFEE

The only coffee grown in the USA comes from Hawaii. A narrow, mountainous strip of land on Hawaii's Kona Coast produces some of the finest coffee in the world, with one of the highest yields – almost 1,200 pounds per acre. There are only 2,600 acres of coffee plantations, virtually all of them in Kona, but they yield a massive 2 million pounds of beans annually.

Coffee was first introduced to Kona in 1828 as an ornamental plant, grown from cuttings taken from a farm in the Manoa Valley on Oahu (the original plants had come from Brazil). Oahu's

soil and climate may have been unsuited to commercial coffee production, but the plants thrived in the volcanic soil on the slopes of Mauna Loa. By 1898 Kona's farmers, mostly British or Americans, were growing coffee on over 6,300 acres and employing Hawaiians to pick the beans. Then other nationalities entered the game, particularly Japanese laborers who, after their sugar plantation contracts expired, began to lease land and plant coffee. By 1979, land under cultivation had dropped to less than 2,000 acres, but recent interest in gourmet beans and higher prices have revitalized the coffee market.

Most Kona coffee is sold in the USA, about 8 percent goes to Japan, and the rest ends up in speciality shops in Canada and Europe. The coffee has a distinctive aroma and taste which, along with its strong regional identity, make it stand out from the competition. Coffee lovers can sample the brew for themselves at the many growers' tasting rooms along the Kona Coffee Belt. Just take a short drive south of Kailua-Kona on Highway 11 down as far as Captain Cook for panoramic views of the coffee plantations and numerous opportunities to sample this delicious beverage for free.

Connoisseur's choice, unique to Hawaii

Sugai Products

PURE KONA COFFEE

KONA COFFEE

100% PURE

EMPORIUM

KING OF COFFEES | Net.Wt. oz. | MADE IN KONA HAWAII, USA

KONA PLANTATION COFFEE COMPANY

KONAGROVE

SINCE 1910

NET WT

100% PURE KONA COFFEE

KEALAKEKUA, HAWAII

Thurston Lava Tube

THURSTON LAVA TUBE

When a river of lava flows rapidly downhill, the top and side surfaces cool, leaving a crust under which molten lava continues to flow. The resulting empty channel is called a lava tube. Lorrin Thurston was a member of the expedition that originally discovered this lava tube in Volcanoes National Park. To reach it, a path descends quite steeply from the parking lot on Crater Rim Road. The walk from there is easy and quite beautiful, with a prehistoric fern forest enveloping the trail. Negotiating the tunnel takes about 10 minutes, through narrow passages that open out into big chambers – a very worthwhile excursion, but not for the claustrophobic.
Volcanoes National Park, off Highway 11. Tel: (808) 967–7311. Open: daily 8:30am–5pm. Admission charge for the park.

KOHALA COWBOYS

Early European visitors to the Big Island brought goats, sheep and cows as gifts to Kamehameha I. The creatures thrived on the lush vegetation and soon escaped the low stone wall enclosures built by the Hawaiians. Within a few years their numbers had so multiplied that the island was in serious danger of becoming denuded of vegetation, both wild and cultivated.

John Palmer Parker, an enterprising and energetic New Englander who arrived in 1809, agreed with Kamehameha that in return for a homestead he would get the cattle under control. This was the start of the Parker Ranch. The original two acres given to Parker in Kohala developed into almost a quarter of a million acres, and today 50,000 head of cattle roam the range.

The first cowboys Parker brought over were Spanish-American, and the Hawaiians, having no 's' in their language, called them *paniolo* (a corruption of *español*). Later, Portuguese were brought over to help, and with them came the small guitar that the Hawaiians adopted and called the ukulele.

Hawaiians were quick to pick up the riding and roping skills of the Europeans, which have flourished down the decades. Today, Parker Ranch cowboys represent most ethnic groups on the island. Their cowboy culture is alive and well, and demonstrated for the public every year at rodeos throughout the state.

WAIMEA

This frequently misty and wet little town is as far from the typical image of Hawaii as possible. At 2,670 feet, it nestles in rolling green hills below the snowy summit of Mauna Kea, much cooler than the coastal resorts. Waimea makes a refreshing change, in more ways than one. The town is virtually run by the Parker Ranch, whose 225,000 acres surround it. Hawaiian cowboys, called _paniolos_ (see box), give a distinctly Old West flavor to the place in their cowboy boots and hats. There are several excellent craft shops and restaurants.

The postal name for this town is Kamuela, to distinguish it from Waimea on Kauai, but here on the Big Island 'Kamuela' and 'Waimea' are one and the same.

WAIPIO VALLEY

One of Hawaii's most magical experiences is a visit to the remote Waipio Valley.

This was always a place of great spiritual significance and continues to be so today. The Waipio Valley appears to be an overgrown jungle, but a handful of houses are scattered along the valley floor. Once, this was the largest cultivated valley in Hawaii, and every food known to Hawaiians flourished here. From the overlook outside Kukuihaele, you can still see taro fields and fish ponds 1,000 feet below. Even today, the valley could supply the whole population of the island if necessary.

Only one very steep road descends into Waipio, and it is dangerous to attempt it without four-wheel drive. Most people hike down (far easier than hiking up) or go down on the Waipio Valley Shuttle (see page 142).
End of Highway 240, in the north of the island.

The serene, relatively inaccessible Waipio Valley has always been abundantly fertile

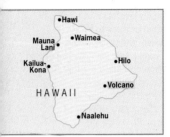

Kilauea Iki Crater

Nowhere in the world is it as easy to experience the awesome forces of an active volcano as on the Big Island. Hawaii Volcanoes National Park offers the serious hiker numerous itineraries that can take anything from a few minutes to several days. One of the most accessible, and also most interesting, is the walk down into Kilauea Iki Crater. It gives a perfect introduction to the main features of this active volcanic area. All walks in the park are potentially serious undertakings, and hikers should be in good physical condition. Wear sturdy, closed-toe walking shoes, not sandals, and long pants. Lava fields are hot and shadeless, so take sunscreen and at least two pints of water per person. Stay on marked trails. Avoid cliffs, earthcracks and steam vents, all of which can be very unstable. Volcanic fumes can be highly toxic, and anyone with respiratory or heart problems should avoid steam vents. *Allow 2 hours for the 4-mile loop. Strenuous walking.*

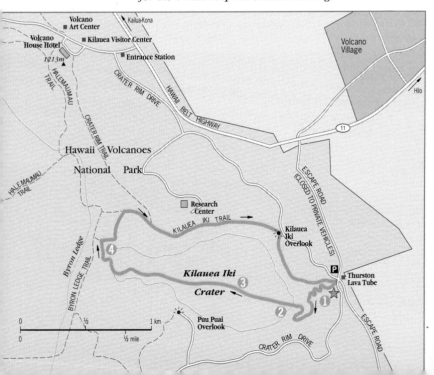

Plant life braves a hostile environment

After entering the park, turn left into Crater Rim Drive. The first stop on the left, after about 2 miles, is Kilauea Iki Overlook. Continue ½ mile to the Thurston Lava Tube parking lot. The trail starts directly across the road from the lava tube entrance. Do not leave valuables in the car, as theft is a common occurrence even in such a pristine wilderness.

1 THROUGH A HAPU'U FOREST

Walk down through a giant fern forest, where hikers are dwarfed by the huge hapu'u fern, which is found nowhere else on earth. A ½-mile switchback trail descends 400 feet through this lush foliage to the edge of the crater. Alongside the ferns are many plants indigenous to the Hawaiian Islands, and with luck you may see birds like the brilliant scarlet Hawaiian honeycreeper or maybe even a Hawaiian owl.

2 LAVA FROM 1959

The trail leads down to a chaos of lava that was pushed up during the spectacular eruption of Kilauea Iki in November 1959. Tread carefully for a few yards. Falls onto lava can cause nasty cuts.

3 THE WARM CRATER FLOOR

The floor of the crater is like a lunar surface, with a trail leading across the middle in almost total desolation. Near the edge a few small plants tentatively try to establish themselves, pushing up through the black surface, but before long there is nothing but an expanse of still-warm lava and an increasing number of steam vents – a sobering reminder of the restless and terrible force beneath your feet.

4 ASCENT TO THE RIM

At the far side of the crater floor, the trail loops round to the right and climbs up steeply through more giant ferns back to the Thurston Lava Tube parking lot.

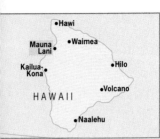

South Kohala Coast

The ancient Ala Kahakai Trail stretches 175 miles from Upolu Point in north Kohala to Hawaii Volcanoes National Park. It follows the Kohala Coast down past many of the finest resorts in Hawaii. The weather along the south Kohala Coast is among the best and most consistent in the Islands – which is perhaps why Hawaiians, from earliest times to more recent royalty, have gravitated to this sun-drenched coast. The walk can get very hot, so bring a supply of water. *Allow 90 minutes.*

Take the Mauna Lani Drive off Queen Kaahumanu Highway. Follow the signs to the Ritz-Carlton. Just before the hotel, turn right into a small road that crosses a golf course, to Holoholokai Beach Park. At the end is a paved parking lot; at the inland end is a footpath leading to Puako Petroglyph Archeological Preserve.

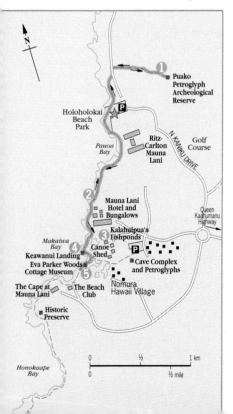

1 PUAKO PETROGLYPH ARCHEOLOGICAL PRESERVE

The walk to the petroglyphs passes through dense scrub for about half a mile; this section is fairly rough and usually very hot. At the start is an interpretative display with reproductions of the petroglyphs from which to make rubbings. (Anyone who may find the walk too exhausting will get a good idea of the petroglyphs from this opening exhibit.) Towards the end the trail crosses a rough road. A short distance beyond is a viewing platform from which to see the 3,000 petroglyphs that cover smooth slabs of lava. This is the largest concentration of petroglyphs in the Islands, and one of the finest.

In the past, visitors have unwittingly damaged these important cultural relics. Please be careful and do not walk on

These simple linear petroglyphs were carved in the ancient lava by the island's early inhabitants

the petroglyphs or take rubbings here.
Retrace the Trail.

2 MAUNA LANI BUNGALOWS

Just before the Mauna Lani Hotel there are three bungalows set back from the Trail. These ultra-exclusive Mauna Lani Bungalows are popular with Hollywood celebrities, and it is not unusual to spot the likes of Rod Stewart or Kevin Costner relaxing by their private swimming pools.
Continue past the Mauna Lani Hotel.

3 KALAHUIPUA'A FISHPONDS

To the left of the Trail are several saltwater lagoons that were used as fishponds by the ancient *ali'i* (chiefs). These were a unique invention of the Hawaiians. True aquaculture did not occur anywhere else in Polynesia. The largest pond covers 5 acres and is one of the best examples of a functioning Hawaiian fishpond.
Continue a short distance south along the coast.

4 KEAWANUI LANDING

King Kamehameha I had a canoe and a small village here. A replica of a canoe shed, which houses a full-scale model of an outrigger fishing canoe, marks the landing site.
Cross a small bridge and continue a short distance.

5 EVA PARKER WOODS COTTAGE MUSEUM

This small museum illustrates the lives of Kalahuipua'a's earliest inhabitants. The cottage, originally built in the 1920s, was relocated here to house the museum.
Return to Holoholokai Beach Park along the same path.

Hilo Town

Although it's the second biggest city in the state, Hilo is very much a small, friendly town. Unlike Honolulu, it has a strong tropical ambience, complete with rusty red and green corrugated roofs and peeling paint. This walk gives a good introduction to the architecture of the old downtown commercial center of Hilo. *Allow 1 hour.*

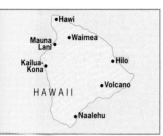

Hilo is not a major tourist destination, and parking is rarely a problem. Parking meters are cheap and plentiful. Start in Kalakaua Park on Kinoole Street and cross Kalakaua Street.

1 OLD POLICE STATION

The building was designed in 1932 by Frank Arakawa to resemble a Hawaiian *hale* (native house) of the 1800s. The police moved out in 1979 and the East Hawaii Cultural Center moved in, supporting local arts and sponsoring festivals, workshops and performances.
Continue down Kalakaua Street.

2 HAWAIIAN TELEPHONE COMPANY BUILDING

The architect C. W. Dickey developed Hawaiian Regional Architecture, which draws on Mediterranean/California Mission style and the Hawaiian *hale*. This 1920s building

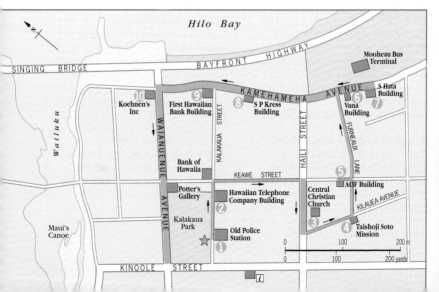

is typical of Dickey's eclectic vision.
Continue down Kalakaua Street, turn right into Keawe Street and right again into Haili Street.

3 CENTRAL CHRISTIAN CHURCH

At one time there were five churches on Haili Street. Now only three remain. This small Victorian-style church was built for the Portuguese-speaking community in the early 1900s, and its appearance has not altered from that time.
Continue up Haili Street and turn left into Kilauea Avenue.

4 TAISHOJI SOTO MISSION

On the right of the street is a mission established by Zen Buddhists in 1913.
Continue down Kilauea Avenue, turn left down Furneaux Lane and left into Keawe Street.

5 AOF BUILDING

The Ancient Order of Foresters still uses these premises, which were built in 1925 in Renaissance Revival style. King Kalakaua was a member of the order.
Continue down Furneaux Lane to Kamehameha Avenue. Turn right.

6 VANA BUILDING

Another Mediterranean-influenced building.
Continue right along Kamehameha Avenue.

7 S HATA BUILDING

This was built in Renaissance Revival style in 1912 by the Hata family, of Japanese descent. During World War II it was confiscated by the government as property belonging to aliens. It was bought back by the family after the war and is still run as a family business.

Turn back along Kamehameha Avenue and walk past Haili Street.

8 S P KRESS BUILDING

When this was built in 1932, it was Hilo's first introduction to Art Deco. The building is best viewed from across the street by the parking lot.
Continue on to Kalakaua Street.

9 FIRST HAWAIIAN BANK BUILDING

This is another of architect C. W. Dickey's buildings. It was built in 1930 and survived two massive *tsunamis* (tidal waves) in 1946 and 1960.
Continue to the corner of Waianuenue Avenue.

10 KOEHNEN'S INC

The Hackfield Company built this Renaissance Revival building in 1910. The Koehnens bought it in 1957 and carried out extensive renovations, but wisely kept the koa wood walls inside and the ohia wood floors.
Walk up Waianuenue Avenue for two blocks to Kinoole Street. Kalakaua Park is on the left.

Kailua-Kona

Kailua-Kona was once a favourite destination for the Hawaiian royal family. Today, the important historic sites are intermingled with shopping malls, tourist shops and restaurants. This walk follows Ali'i Drive along the waterfront. Parking is always a problem in this small town, but space is usually available in the parking lot behind King Kamehameha's Kona Beach Hotel. Parking validation – which reduces the parking fee considerably – is available by patronizing the hotel's restaurants or shops, which are no more expensive than anywhere else in town.

From the parking lot, walk behind the hotel to Kailua Pier.

1 AHU'ENA HEIAU AND KAMAKAHONU COMPOUND

King Kamehameha I ruled Hawaii from these grounds from 1812 to 1819, and this was where he was to spend his last days. When he died his bones were prepared in accordance with ancient ritual inside the main temple before being taken to a secret burial place. The reconstruction of the *heiau* was initiated by Kamehameha himself, although the buildings you see today are of much more recent origin.

2 KAILUA PIER

The waters off Kona provide some of the world's best big-game fishing, and this pier is the center of the action during the marlin season (see page 105). Fishing boats are in and out all

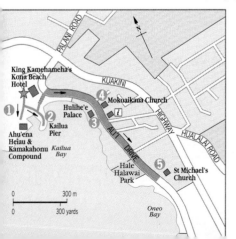

day, and it's not unusual to see a proud fisherman standing by a 300-pound marlin dangling from the scales by its tail. For the less ambitious, a rod and line from the edge of the pier can put a tasty dinner on the table.
Follow Ali'i Drive along the seafront for 200 yards.

3 HULIHE'E PALACE

Overlooking Kailua Bay, this palace was built from coral and lava in 1838 by the first Governor of Hawaii, John Adams Kuakini, who also happened to be King

Ahu'ena Heiau, where the old order of *kapu* was destroyed after Kamehameha's death

> **Hulihe'e Palace** – 75–5718 Ali'i Drive. Tel: (808) 329–1877. Open: daily 9am–4pm. Admission charge.
> **Mokuaikaua Church** – open: daily 6am–6pm.

with ohia wood beams and koa wood pews and pulpit. The orientation of the building allows prevailing winds to pass through the length of the church to provide natural air conditioning. Inside there is an excellent model of the brig *Thaddeus*, a Polynesian navigational star chart and several historical paintings. *Continue along Ali'i Drive. On either side of the road there are small shopping developments that cater to every taste, with a sprinkling of cafés and restaurants, most of which make a pleasant stop even if the food is rarely memorable.*

Kamehameha's brother-in-law. It was used as a summer retreat by the royal family until 1916. The Daughters of Hawaii now operate the palace as a museum. Most of the koa wood furniture is authentic and includes a massive dining table made from one solid koa log and the four-poster bed belonging to Queen Kapiolani (see page 105). *Walk directly across Ali'i Drive.*

4 MOKUAIKAUA CHURCH
The church's 112-foot steeple is the tallest structure in town and has been Kailua's landmark since it was built in 1836 (see page 109). This is reputedly the oldest church in Hawaii. It was constructed out of lava stones using a mortar containing crushed coral and kukui nut oil. The interior was finished

5 ST MICHAEL'S CHURCH
On the *mauka* (mountain-facing) side of Ali'i Drive is the oldest Catholic church outside of Honolulu, built in 1840. *Return back along Ali'i Drive.*

A little grass hut in St Michael's cemetery marks the site of an earlier thatched chapel

Madame Pele

The ancestral religion may have been thrown out by Queen Kapiolani in the 1820s, but one of its deities lives on. Pele, the goddess of fire, is as real to many Hawaiians today as she was 500 years ago – and she is equally feared.

According to legend, Pele came to Hawaii to fight her cruel sister Na Maka o Kaha'i, the goddess of the sea. She first went to Niihau but was driven out. This continued down the chain of islands until she arrived on the Big Island, where she made her home deep in the high mountains. She appears before eruptions from her Kilauea home, sometimes as a beautiful young woman but more often as a wrinkled old hag. Whatever her form, she is unpredictable and tempestuous. She demands respect. Old Hawaiians used to say of Kilauea: "Step

lightly, for you are on holy ground."

So infectious is superstition about Pele that every week the local post office receives parcels of volcanic rocks, sometimes as many as 30 a day, collected by repentant visitors to Volcanoes National Park. They claim that the rocks brought them bad luck and ask that they be returned to Pele, who is the rightful owner. The post office solemnly carries out this duty. Rumor has it that this particular superstition was invented by a tour bus driver who was fed up with tourists' dirty old rocks messing up his bus – but is it worth taking the chance?

Pele is said to occasionally appear by the roadside at night asking for a lift. A more reliable way of seeing Madame Pele is to visit the Volcano House next to Volcanoes National Park headquarters, where a bas-relief of the fiery female appropriately adorns the fireplace.

The fire goddess, Volcanoes National Park

GETTING AWAY FROM IT ALL

... everything was deuced romantic – a warm starry night and the scent of oleanders all about – you know how it is. Honolulu.

Getting Away From It All

*A*lthough the Hawaiian Islands attract over 6 million tourists a year, it is still possible to escape the crowds and experience a laid-back lifestyle that has hardly changed for decades. Abandon the high-rise resorts of Maui, take a few minutes' journey by air, and return to Earth to meet a totally different Hawaii, on the islands of Molokai and Lanai (see map on pages 78–9). On any given day, there are over 100,000 tourists in the state, but only a handful of them find their way over to these quiet backwaters.

Lanai, the sixth largest island in Hawaii, was once the heart of the Hawaiian pineapple industry. James Dole bought the entire island in 1922, built Lanai City and established himself as the pineapple king. The company still owns the island, although the emphasis has shifted from pineapples to tourism.

There are only three paved roads on the island, and there is none of the lush landscape that is so appealing on the other islands. Lanai, stark and barren, nevertheless has two of the finest hotels in

Hawaii. The deluxe Lodge at Koele sits high above Lanai City, and the almost constant swirling mists give a feeling of the Scottish Highlands rather than a tropical island. Here is the ultimate getaway.

Molokai, the state's fifth largest island, is more down-to-earth, a place of peaceful rural solitude, the Hawaii of yesteryear where visitors are still something of a novelty. There are no posh hotels, and facilities for tourists are minimal. Fewer than 7,000 people live on the island, which still hasn't a single traffic light.

The scenery of Molokai can be dramatic. The highest peak is almost 5,000 feet above sea level, and the cliffs on the north coast are the highest in the world, plunging over 1,600 feet into the Pacific. On this same north coast is the Kalaupapa Peninsula, infamous for its leper colony, and one of the most moving places to visit in all Hawaii.

MOLOKAI
Halawa Valley
At the far eastern tip of this slipper-shaped island, lush vegetation takes over from the rolling ranchlands of the west. A tortuous coastal road winds past secluded

View at the end of an often slippery trail: Moaula Falls plunging into a deep cool pool

beaches against a backdrop of wild mountains. The road ends in the beautiful Halawa Valley. A dirt road leads to the delightful Halawa Beach Park, where facilities are primitive (no camping is allowed).

During the drive down into the valley, two dramatic waterfalls are visible in the distance surrounded by sheer mountain walls, and anyone capable of undertaking it should make the two-mile hike to the swimming hole at the foot of 250-foot Moaula Falls. A rough field is operated as "security parking" by an old Gauguin-like character, who sells drinks and basic snacks from a shack on the site. His outrageously high parking fee includes a sheet with directions to the falls.

The trail is relatively easy and winds gently through orchards, ancient Hawaiian home sites and lush tropical vegetation to the inviting pool under the cascading falls. Colored markers make it hard to get lost. The upper Hipuapua Falls can be reached by a precipitously steep trail that is difficult to find.

Hale o Lono Harbor
Most of the land in western Molokai is owned and operated by Molokai Ranch. At the far western tip of Molokai there is a small natural harbor and secluded beach that must be one of the most isolated in Hawaii. It can only be reached across land owned by Molokai Ranch via a dirt road with a gate. The gate is locked, but the key, and directions, can be collected from the Molokai Ranch office in Maunaloa. Rental cars are not officially allowed on dirt roads, and the red dust of Molokai is an obvious give-away. Anyone daring to risk the wrath of the car rental agents is advised to hose down the car before returning it to the airport!
Molokai Ranch – tel: (808) 552–2767.

Hale o Lono: every September in Aloha Week, outrigger canoes race from here to Oahu

Skimmed by cloud, the highest sea cliffs in the world pierce the Pacific at Kalaupapa

Iliiliopae Heiau

Hawaii's second largest temple lies on private land just off the main highway through Molokai. The massive platform and terraces of volcanic rock, overgrown by tropical vegetation, were once the scene of human sacrifice and sorcery. The site exudes atmosphere even on a bright, sunny day. Access is restricted and the place is difficult to find without a guide. However, a horse-drawn tour includes the *heiau* together with visits to other nearby attractions.
Molokai Wagon Rides, Hoolehua.
Tel: (808) 558–8380.

Kalaupapa

A visit to Kalaupapa is one of the most emotional and rewarding experiences anywhere in the Hawaiian Islands. In 1865, the Hawaiian government exiled lepers to this isolated peninsula in the shadow of the world's highest sea cliffs. They were abandoned with few provisions and no shelter, and thrown into a lawless, despairing society. In 1873 a Belgian Catholic priest, Father Damien Joseph de Veuster, came alone to serve these sufferers of Hansen's disease as priest, doctor, builder and tireless advocate, persuading the government to provide supplies of food, clothing, timber for housing and, eventually, a proper water supply. Father Damien, "Apostle of the Lepers," died of the disease himself 16 years later among the outcasts whose lives he had transformed (see also page 39).

You can visit the settlement, where about 100 sufferers of Hansen's disease still live – though without coercion, now that the disease is treatable – either by plane or by hiking down 1,664 feet from Palaau State Park. Once on the peninsula, you must take a guided tour operated by Damien Tours. No children under the age of 16 are allowed.
Damien Tours. Tel: (808) 567–6171.

Kaunakakai

This is the only town of note on Molokai. The Molokai Visitor Center is here on Highway 460 opposite the main petrol station. Kanemitsu's Bakery, on the main street, has operated for over 70 years; they bake some of the best bread in the Islands and also have a simple cafeteria which opens for breakfast every day at 6am. Near a pier are the remains of Kamehameha V's summer house, looking more like a derelict building site.

The road heading west out of Kaunakakai, called Church Row, is lined with places of worship for seven different denominations. On Sundays all of them are filled with locals. Opposite Church Row is the island's biggest coconut grove, planted by King Kamehameha V in 1860.

Molokai Ranch

Molokai Ranch, the second biggest in the state at over 50,000 acres, promises to be the biggest visitor attraction on the island. Its main attraction is the recently renovated Molokai Ranch Wildlife Conservation Park. The 400-acre park specializes in hoofed animals from round the world, including giraffe, zebra, eland and oryx. The habitats are virtually identical to the animals' natural habitat, and environmental awareness is emphasized. Two-hour safari van tours are accompanied by knowledgeable naturalist guides. At the end, visitors can hand-feed the giraffe and other animals. It's a photographer's field day.
Outfitters Center, Maunaloa. Tel: (808) 552–2767.

Palaau State Park

This 34-acre park has full facilities for picnicking, including toilets. There are several easy hiking trails, but its best feature is the near-aerial view, from 1,600 feet, of the spectacular Kalaupapa Peninsula. An easy 10-minute walk from the road-head parking lot leads to the Lookout. Clouds often swirl round here, but be patient – a break in the clouds reveals a breathtaking view of Kalaupapa, and the tallest sea cliffs in the world.

In the grounds of St Philomena's Church, Kalaupapa, lie the remains of Father Damien

Papohaku Beach

Papohaku is the biggest expanse of beach on Molokai. Over 2 miles long and 100 yards wide, this magnificent white-sand beach is one of the great undiscovered treasures of Hawaii. The modest facilities include toilets and basic picnic needs, and although camping is not officially allowed, tents are often seen here. It is hard to believe that, in one of the world's great tourist destinations, there can be an outstandingly beautiful beach that is so little used. There is a serious downside, however: currents are very strong throughout the year, and extreme caution is required when swimming. *Just off the road past Kalaukoi Resort.*

Phallic Rock

Surrounded by a grove of ironwood trees in Palaau State Park stands a surprisingly lifelike, 6-foot-tall phallus-shaped rock, its realism enhanced over the years by some carving. Ka'uleonanahoa, as the rock is known in Hawaiian, is reputed to cure infertility in women. *Palaau State Park, end of Highway 470. The rock is a 10-minute walk from the parking lot at the end of the road into the park.*

Purdy's Nut Farm

Just off the road leading out from Hoolehua is a small macadamia nut operation that should not be missed. Unlike most of the big commercial macadamia nut growers, there is no pressure to make sales. In fact, there is very little for sale. Nuts, obviously, and macadamia flower honey, but not a T-shirt in sight! This is a very small-scale farm, virtually a one-man operation. The enthusiastic Mr Purdy takes great delight in showing visitors the process of macadamia nut farming. *Lihipali Avenue, Hoolehua. Tel: (808) 567–6601. Open: Monday to Saturday 9:30am–3:30pm, Sunday by appointment only. Free.*

R. W. Meyer Sugar Mill

A new museum displaying artifacts of old Molakai and the Meyer family has recently opened next to the R. W. Meyer Sugar Mill. The sugar mill has become one of the exhibits of the museum, fully restored to its original condition with a mule-driven cane-crusher, copper clarifiers and an 1878 steam engine. This is one of the best examples in Hawaii of a genuine sugar mill operation. *Route 470, Kualapuu. Tel: (808) 567–6436. Open: Monday to Saturday 10am–2pm. Closed: state holidays. Admission charge.*

St Joseph's Church

This simple church on the road from Kaunakakai to Halawa was built by Father Damien Joseph de Veuster in 1876 (see pages 39 and 130) and named for his patron, St Joseph, on whose feast day he first arrived in Hawaii. A statue of the priest stands at the side of the church.

Phallic Rock protrudes in Palaau State Park

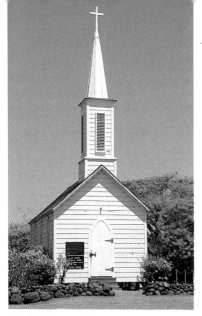

The little Church of St Joseph, built by Father Damien Joseph de Veuster

LANAI
Club Lanai

Most people visit this beachfront resort as day-trippers from Lahaina on Maui. A full range of beach activities is offered, including snorkelling. All meals are provided and there is a full bar. Don't expect to see anything of Lanai, however. Club Lanai is isolated on the eastern shore of the island at the end of a very long dirt road. Few people actually staying on the island ever make it round this far – and Lanai's two deluxe hotels far outshine this limited facility.

Club Lanai. Tel: (808) 871–1144. Admission charge. The Club operates a catamaran that leaves Pier 4 in Lahaina at 7:15am and returns at 3pm.

Garden of the Gods

An old pineapple road out of Lanai City rapidly disintegrates into a rough dirt track and, after about 7 miles, passes through a bizarre landscape of weirdly shaped boulders and intensely colored earth. It is a unique and strange environment, unlike anything else in the Pacific islands.

Polihua Road (Awalua Highway), Lanai City.

At sunrise and sunset, colors and shapes are transformed at the Garden of the Gods

Keomuku

Cutting across the island, a paved road (Highway 44, the Keomuku Highway) climbs up to Lanai City, then descends in a series of hairpin bends to the north shore. A dirt road follows the shoreline past Shipwreck Beach (see below), and after about 6 miles you'll see a solitary church dating from 1903 which marks the site of the ghost town of Keomuku. Tall coconut trees grow where once there was a busy community centered on a sugar company. Crumbling stone walls are all that remain of its grand homes, but a certain eerie beauty lingers about the place.

Lanai City

Lanai City is still the sleepy little pineapple plantation town it always was, 1,600 feet up in the cool mountain air. Almost all of the island's 2,400 inhabitants live here. The quaint Hotel Lanai is one of only three hotels on the island. There is little else in town apart from general stores, a couple of homely cafés and a small arts and crafts gallery, but you can count on personal service and friendly charm.

Luahiwa Petroglyphs

These remarkable petroglyphs depicting the life of the islanders are some of the finest in Hawaii – and also the most difficult to find. Leaving Lanai City on Route 440, turn left at the first dirt road. Follow the lower road and, after passing a water tank and pipeline, take the left fork. After a sharp curve, several black boulders can be seen above the road. These feature the rock carvings.

Manele Bay

The small harbor here provides a regular ferry service to Lahaina, and chartered catamarans sail over from Maui for picnics by the bay. The deluxe Manele Bay Hotel stands beside the crescent of Hulopoe Beach.

Munro Trail

George Munro, a naturalist from New Zealand, came to Lanai in 1911, replanted areas that had been overgrazed by goats and introduced the Norfolk pine, now a feature of Lanai's high country. This jeep trail climbs for 7 miles to the highest point on the island. In clear weather the trail gives marvellous views of the neighbouring islands. *Drive north on Highway 44 towards Shipwreck Beach. About 1 mile past The Lodge at Koele, turn right onto the paved road that leads to a cemetery in ½ mile. The Trail starts at the left of the cemetery.*

Shipwreck Beach

The rusting remains of an old tanker grounded off the coast can be seen all the way down Route 44 from Lanai City. At the end of the surfaced road, turn left and drive past a few groups of shacks

Charter companies and ferries serving at Manele Bay offer breezy outings

Searching for Niihau's rare tiny shells; below, the rugged shore of Hawaii's last unspoilt island

along a dirt road. Tricky winds co-operated with reefs to give this beach its name, and it's still an excellent area for beachcombing. Just past the parking lot at the end of the dirt road, white markers lead to an area of ancient petroglyphs.

NIIHAU

This is the only island where all the inhabitants are 100 percent pure Hawaiian, with Hawaiian as their first language. The "Forbidden Island" is privately owned by the Robinson family. Until very recently it was off-limits to everyone, including native Hawaiians. The residents of Niihau come and go as they please, but anyone leaving the island to marry is not allowed back. The Robinsons now let visitors fly to the island in their helicopter (no attempt at contact with the local population is allowed). Niihau's scenery is significantly different from its neighbors, and it can be fun searching the beaches for the tiny shells used for the famous Niihau *leis*.
Niihau Helicopters, Kaumakani.
Tel: (808) 335–3500.

ATLANTIS SUBMARINES

Commercial submarines were introduced in Hawaii in 1988, and there are now five in service, on Oahu, Maui and the Big Island. On Oahu the *Atlantis* dives off Waikiki. The natural reef was destroyed long ago, but artificial reefs – including a sunken plane and cargo ship – have replaced it. Shoals of exotic tropical fish swim round these wrecks, and scuba divers can usually be seen keeping them company.

A natural coral garden still exists off Maui, and the submarine explores this fascinating environment as well as underwater volcanic caves. The Kona Coast of the Big Island also has an area of coral gardens, but the big thrill comes in spotting bigger residents like barracuda, marlin or dolphin.

The shuttle ride to the submarine is enjoyable in itself. The submarine, which can descend to 150 feet, stays down for about 50 minutes. The whole trip takes just under 3 hours. Children must be at least 36 inches tall.

All Atlantis Submarines operate daily every hour from 7am to 5pm. On the Big Island: King Kamehameha's Kona Beach Hotel. Tel: (808) 329–6626. Admission charge. On Maui: Lahaina Harbor by the Pioneer Inn. Tel: (808) 667–2224. On Oahu, Hilton Hawaiian Village, Waikiki. Tel: (808) 973–9811.

Above and left: the world beneath the waves explored by submarine

BIRD'S-EYE VIEWS

The islands of Hawaii are perhaps at their most breathtaking when viewed from above. To provide this perspective, helicopter companies have sprouted on the four main islands. Several companies also video-tape the flight and give passengers a souvenir cassette to take home (it can't compete with the magic of the original experience, of course).

On Kauai, the flight over the Na Pali Coast is magnificent, the most beautiful flight in Hawaii. The flight round Oahu shows how much more there is to the island than Honolulu and Waikiki. Returning over Pearl Harbor, you can clearly see the sunken USS *Arizona*. Maui flights generally cover either West Maui or Haleakala and Hana. Mount Haleakala definitely provides the more unusual experience, as the helicopter passes Science City, on the rim of the volcano, and then swoops into the vast crater. But if only one flight can be taken, it should be on the Big Island, over Volcanoes National Park. Passing right over the Kilauea caldera, you peer straight down into the bubbling, red-hot magma, then follow the lava flow till it splutters into the sea, sending up clouds of steam.

Flights on the Big Island leave either from Hilo, Volcano or the Kohala Coast. The Kohala heliport, though convenient, is so distant from Kilauea that the flight involves a lot of "dead time" and costs much more. Using the other heliports allows much more time to explore the park.

It must be said that helicopter rides are inherently dangerous, and several fatal accidents have occurred over the past few years. Generally, however, the small, owner-operated companies have an excellent safety record, with very experienced pilots.

On the Big Island: Island Helicopters, Hilo Airport. Tel: (808) 969–1172. On Kauai: Island Helicopters, Lihue Airport. Tel: (808) 245–8588. On Oahu: Hawaii International Helicopters, Honolulu. Tel: (808) 839–1566.

CRUISE DOWN A VOLCANO

Maui offers the ultimate in effortless cycling. From the top of dormant Haleakala the road drops 10,000 feet in

Helicopter flights offer a uniquely stunning view of Hawaii's dramatic terrain

38 miles, passing through seven different climate zones, from subarctic to subtropical. The downhill cruising operators make sure their van, containing you and your rented cycle, reaches the summit well before sunrise – which, seen from the crater rim, is sublime.

Cruiser Bob's Haleakala Downhill, 99 Hana Highway, Paia. Tel: (808) 667–7717.

Maui Downhill, 199 Dairy Road, Kahului. Tel: (808) 871–2155.

LIFE'S A BEACH

Every island is surrounded by beaches, most of them swarming with an international assortment of sun worshippers. But each island still has a few undiscovered jewels, usually hidden or relatively inaccessible, that the world passes by.

Big Island

Waialea Bay on the South Kohala Coast has a white sand beach extending along the rocky shoreline. Turn off the Kaahumanu Highway at the 69-mile marker. Go about ½ mile on the paved road and turn right into a dirt road at the very bottom of the hill. Take the left fork to the beach.

Kauai

North of Lihue there are several secluded beaches only accessible by hiking down from the main highway. Donkey Beach is a wide curving beach flanked by ironwood trees, hard to find and never crowded. Just before the 12-mile marker on the Kuhio Highway north of Kealia, there is

Join the crowds, or beat them. From top: Mauna Ke..

a cane road on the right. Donkey Beach is about ½ mile down on the left.

Secret Beach, below Kilauea Lighthouse, is very hard to get to and all the more secluded. Turn into Kalihiwai Road off the Kuhio Highway. Take the first dirt road on the right and follow it for about ¼ mile. A steep path leads down from a parking lot.

Lumahai Beach was made famous in the film *South Pacific* as the place where Mitzi Gaynor tried to "wash that man right out of her hair." Black volcanic rocks stand out against the white sand of the beach – unfortunately, swimming here is often extremely dangerous. A steep path leads down to the beach from a lookout point near the 5-mile marker on the Kuhio Highway.

Maui

Slaughterhouse Beach on West Maui looks out over Molokai. It is reached by a steep descent from Route 30 just less than a mile past D. T. Fleming Beach Park.

Stunning Makena Beach lies at the end of the Wailea road. The bigger west-facing section is ideal for watching sunsets, and the adjoining little cove is a nudist beach.

◀ Island; Hamoa, Maui; northeast Kauai coast

Oahu

Hanauma Bay is one of the most popular on the island, but so special that it shouldn't be missed: nearly circular and lined with a narrow, palm-fringed beach. The bay is an underwater park and conservation area, with the best snorkelling and sub-aqua diving on Oahu.

Halona Cove Beach, only just below the main highway, is wedged between Halona Point and Halona Blowhole Lookout. Swim only in gentle seas; rough water here is extremely dangerous.

A WHALE OF A TIME

Look at the works in any Lahaina art gallery and the importance of the whale will be immediately apparent. Lahaina grew up on the whaling industry, and whales are depicted on anything that doesn't move. Fortunately, enough of them were spared to ensure their future in the Pacific Ocean.

Every year from December to May, humpback whales visit Hawaii to escape the harsh Alaska winter and to give birth to their single 2,000-pound calves in the warm Hawaiian waters. At the same time, whale-watching becomes a local preoccupation. Humpbacks are best spotted from Maui and Kauai, where any high vantage point gives a good view of these enormous mammals. For an up-close experience, take a sailboat out to Molokini. Humpbacks like the Molokini atoll, and they seem to like sailboats too.

Whale cruises are also operated by nonprofit organizations like the Pacific Whale Foundation. Their two ships offer three-hour cruises from December to May, and all profits go to research and lobbying.

Pacific Whale Foundation, Kealia Beach Plaza, Kihei, Maui, HI 96753. Tel: (808) 879–8811.

FLORA AND FAUNA

Over a span of 70 million years, animals and plants colonized Hawaii at the rate of about one every 70,000 years. Seeds and spores were carried on to the islands in the jet stream or carried by birds; insects and snails arrived on floating debris. Few mammals were able to cross the vast expanse of the Pacific and, prior to humans, only monk seals and hoary bats succeeded.

Millions of organisms embarked on the voyage, but very few made it and survived in the extremely harsh environment of these volcanic islands. There were no natural enemies here and no competition for food or space, and those that did survive evolved over time into new, better-adapted species. As few as 15 ancestral immigrant birds gave rise to 39 species and 39 subspecies of endemic birds. The 22 species of Hawaiian honeycreeper probably evolved from a single species. Insects, molluscs and ferns evolved in the same way.

From left: the endangered Hawaiian monk seal; the rare nene goose; the king protea; a mixed bunch of natives; the superb silversword

Seed plants flourished. At their peak, more than 1,700 species grew on the Islands. Among the better-known endemic plants are

the acacia koa, several species of hibiscus and the alpine silversword. Inevitably, humans' introduction of insects, animals and exotic plants resulted ultimately in the complete destruction of many native species. Similarly, the extinction of many ground-nesting birds resulted from the introduction of the Indian mongoose, which is now the most commonly seen animal.

Today, several species struggle desperately for survival. The Hawaiian monk seal occurs only on the remote northern islands of the chain, in pitifully small numbers. The nene, the state bird, fights for survival on the brutal lava beds of the Big Island. Much of the unique flora and fauna has disappeared forever, but hopefully, modern conservation efforts will preserve what remains for future generations.

WAIPIO VALLEY

The Waipio Valley on the Big Island is a world unto itself. A steep road only accessible to four-wheel-drive vehicles descends into the valley which, once entered, evokes a strong sense of complete isolation. Here you will find – with difficulty – one of the world's most unusual "hotels." Reaching Linda Beech's Tree House involves driving along a riverbed, along impossibly narrow and overgrown trails, and then fording a river, to arrive at the Tree House at the far end of the valley below a cascading waterfall. The journey alone is remarkable, to say the least.

A more leisurely way to experience the valley is on horseback or on one of the famous Waipio Valley Wagon Tours. An alternative is a jeep tour. This may not be as romantic as horses, but if time is limited, it still gives a good introduction to Waipio.

Linda Beech's Tree House, PO Box 5086, Honokaa. Tel: (808) 775-7160.

Waipio Naalapa Trail Rides. Tel: (808) 775-0419.
Waipio Valley Shuttle and Tours. Tel: (808) 775-7121.
Waipio Valley Wagon Tours. Tel: (808) 775-9518.

ZODIACS TO NA PALI

The sight of Kauai's Na Pali Coast is dramatic from either land or air, but from the sea the rugged green cliffs take on a whole new dimension. Captain Zodiac (aka Clancy Greff) operates a fleet of rubber Zodiac rafts that take over 10,000 adventurous visitors a year out to brave the waves of Na Pali. The rafts leave from Tunnels Beach at Haena and usually go as far as a remote deserted beach called Nualolo Kai, where the clear waters are calm enough for diving.

Captain Zodiac Expeditions, PO Box 456, Hanalei, Kauai, HI 96714. Tel: (808) 826-9371.

Left: Tree House view of Waipio
Below: Na Pali coast

DIRECTORY

I had fancied that in going to the Sandwich Islands, I was going to an uncivilized, heathen place. Imagine my disappointment at finding an ordinary looking city, with pavements and electric lights and telephones all over the place.

LILIAN LELAND
Travelling Alone, A Woman's Journey Round the World, 1890

Shopping

*E*very designer shop imaginable can be found on the Islands, from Louis Vuitton to Cartier, and these are patronized primarily by Japanese visitors. But there are plenty of other places for shoppers whose pockets may not be quite as deep. The free *This Week* and *Spotlight Gold* publications, which appear weekly on all the islands, have extensive listings of shops, current shopping opportunities and discount coupons. It pays to do your homework, particularly when looking for cameras and electronic goods.

Honolulu

The **Ala Moana Shopping Center** is the biggest in the state and reputedly the world's largest "open-air" shopping center. It has over 200 shops, ranging from Woolworth's and Sears to Gucci and Chanel. The **Honolulu Book Shop** (tel: 808 941–2274), Hawaii's best bookstore, is here too. In theory, all your shopping needs could be satisfied with this one stop. It would be a pity, however, to miss some of the other opportunities to shop.

Waikiki

The **Royal Hawaiian Shopping Center** on Kalakaua Avenue has three interconnecting, four-story buildings. The **Waikiki Shopping Plaza** (2270 Kalakaua Avenue) has six floors of shops

and restaurants. Both offer a very wide selection of goods, but usually at tourist prices. **King's Village** (Kaulani Avenue) recalls the Victorian influence on Hawaii's monarchy, and has about as much authenticity as many of the goods on sale there. At the other end of Waikiki, the **Rainbow Bazaar** at Hilton Hawaiian Village provides good souvenir and clothes shopping without ever having to leave the resort. On a humbler scale, the **International Market Place** (2330 Kalakaua Avenue) has several stalls under a spreading banyan tree. It's ideal for browsing, but don't expect to find any bargains or brilliant quality.

Other islands

A few shops on the other islands are worthy of mention. On Kauai, **Kong Lung Co** (tel: 808 828–1822) in Kilauea sells furniture, clothing and jewelry of the highest standard; the North Shore location belies the sophistication of this treasure house. In Waimea on the Big Island, the **Gallery of Great Things** (tel: 808 885–7706) in Parker Square has wonderful collectables from the South Pacific; many items are of museum quality. Also here is **Cook's Discoveries** (tel: 808 885–3633), specializing in the very finest Hawaiian-made products, from Waipio _poi_ to _palaka_ umbrellas with _koa_ handles. This charming shop, in a historic building, has the welcoming atmosphere of a home. On Molokai, in the one-street town of Maunaloa, the **Big Wind Kite Factory** (tel: 808 522–2364) has kites of every shape and color, and the adjoining shop sells items collected on the owner's travels through Asia.

Left: a shady sidewalk passes colorful shops in the quaint artists' colony of Paia, Maui

Memories are made of this: beer mugs by the million recall the popular ice-cold drink

Convenience stores

ABC Discount Stores are ubiquitous in the Islands. In Waikiki alone there are 28. They sell a wide range of goods from foodstuffs to suntan lotion to souvenirs, but don't take the word "discount" too literally. They also have long opening hours. For 24-hour, 365-day-a-year service, the **7-Eleven** chain is island-wide, with a good range of essential foodstuffs and sometimes hot snacks and drinks.

Souvenirs

CORAL AND SHELLS

Pink, black and gold coral from Hawaiian waters are cut, polished and set into jewelry. In Waikiki, **Duke's Lane** between Kalakaua and Kuhio Avenues is filled with stalls selling all kinds of jewelry; try bartering for a better price. In downtown Honolulu, **Maui Divers** is a very slick commercial operation offering free transportation from any hotel and a free tour of their factory – interesting, well presented, and ending in a large showroom/shop.

Shells, surprisingly, are not all that common on Hawaii's beaches. They are frequently used in place of flowers to make *leis*, and the finest, from the "Forbidden Island" of Niihau, are made from thousands of tiny shells and cost thousands of dollars. A wide range of shells and shell jewelry can be seen at **Island Shells** in the Ala Moana Center (tel: 808 947–3313).

FOODSTUFFS

Highly regarded by *aficionados*, Kona coffee has seen a resurgence in popularity. Beans can be bought at the many coffee estates along the Kona Coast, but most speciality food and coffee shops have a good selection.

Macadamia nuts – plain, roasted or covered in chocolate – are one of the most popular Hawaiian gifts. They are on sale everywhere from ABC Discount Stores to Woolworth's.

Roadside shell stand in Haleiwa, Oahu

CLOTHING

The quintessential Hawaiian look – featuring migraine-inducing flower prints – is yours for the price of an *aloha* shirt or *muumuu* dress (the voluminous *muumuu* is particularly popular with women with a fuller figure). One of the biggest outlets is **Hilo Hattie**, with shops on all the main islands (listed in the telephone directory). They provide free transportation from major hotels, greet customers with a shell *lei*, offer free pineapple juice and have one of the most extensive ranges of *aloha* shirts and *muumuus* in the Islands. They also stock a very wide range of other Hawaiian souvenirs and foods – perfect for present-shopping in one fell swoop. Curiously, old *aloha* shirts from the '30s and '40s have become collectors' items, and several shops are now specializing in them.

For something a bit more conservative, eel skin made into purses, briefcases and jackets, as well as the usual wallets and belts, can be found at quite good prices at shops throughout the Islands, though it has now become somewhat *passé*.

OLD PHOTOGRAPHS

Historic prints are a wonderful and inexpensive souvenir. The archives at the **Bishop Museum** (tel: 808 847–3511) contain half a million old photographs of Hawaii which, for a fee, they will make into a print. The **State of Hawaii Archives** (tel: 808 548–2355) have a similar service, although its collection is much smaller.

ARTS AND CRAFTS

Galleries are everywhere; unfortunately, good arts and crafts are not. Most of the so-called art galleries sell marine art that

Big Wind Kite Factory, Maunaloa, Molokai

bears a closer resemblance to cartoons than to fine painting, but nevertheless manages to make the artists very rich. For more substantial works, the **Pegge Hopper Gallery** (1164 Nuuanu Avenue, Honolulu, tel: 808 524–1160) has an ongoing exhibition of works by this renowned Hawaiian artist. The **Gateway Gallery** (1050 Nuuanu Avenue, tel: 808 521–6863) also exhibits paintings and sculpture by several of Hawaii's leading artists.

The **Academy Shop** at the Honolulu Academy of Arts (tel: 808 523–1493) has an impressive collection of crafts by Hawaiian artists, as does **Shop Pacifica** at the Bishop Museum (tel: 808 848–4148). The **Nohea Gallery** in the Ward Warehouse (tel: 808 599–7927) has an eclectic collection of crafts by Hawaiians, including ceramics, glass, prints and jewelry.

Entertainment

*F*or a major tourist destination, Hawaii has a disappointingly narrow range of entertainment. Outside of Honolulu, the pickings are particularly slim. Apart from cinemas the only other diversion is likely to be the ubiquitous Polynesian show or bar music. Comprehensive listings of what's available can be found in newspapers, particularly in the entertainment section of the *Honolulu Advertiser* or *Honolulu Star-Bulletin*'s "Weekend Pass." Information can also be found in the free weekly publications that are on every street corner, although they often list only their advertisers. *This Week* and *Spotlight's Gold* series are produced for each of the four main islands. *Honolulu Magazine* has a good Calendar of Events. The Arts Council of Hawaii (tel: 808 524–7120) publishes a monthly guide to cultural events.

Among the best entertainment values in Honolulu are the free concerts at the Waikiki Shell. Details of these can be found in either of the local daily newspapers. Every May 1st, the Brothers Cazimero play to capacity crowds sitting on the grass in the warm Hawaiian air. What better way could there be to listen to great music?

POLYNESIAN SHOWS

Every island has its own variation of the Polynesian revue, from the grand extravaganza to more modest performances. They all tend to have the same formula: grass-skirted Tahitian maidens swinging their hips, Samoan fire dancers and the Maori *poi* dance. Every *luau* will have an interpretation of this theme, and make up for in enthusiasm what it lacks in authenticity.

Drums of the Pacific
Hyatt Regency Maui, 200 Nohea Kai Drive, Lahaina, Maui. Tel: (808) 667–4420.

Kona Hilton Polynesian Luau
Kona Hilton Resort–Coconut Grove, 75–5852 Alii Drive, Kailua-Kona, Hawaii. Tel: (808) 329–3111.

Polynesian Cultural Center
This is the ultimate South Seas spectacular. Pure Las Vegas.
Kamehameha Highway, Laie, Oahu. Tel: (808) 293–3333.

Royal Luau
Royal Waikoloan Resort, Waikoloa, South Kohala, Hawaii. Tel: (808) 885–6789.

Show time at the shops: Ala Moana Center

Sheraton's Spectacular Polynesian Revue
Sheraton Princess Kaiulani Hotel, 120 Kaiulani Avenue, Honolulu, Oahu. Tel: (808) 971–5305.

DINNER SHOWS

Several Waikiki hotels present shows with the option of dinner or cocktails before the performance. The dinner shows are often surprisingly good value; even if the menus are limited, the food is delicious. The standard of most of the shows can leave a lot to be desired, but the audiences, who tend to be on the mature side, are nevertheless appreciative.

The perennially popular crooner draws large adoring crowds

The Brothers Cazimero

This pair is without question the finest act in town. The range of music produced by just two men with a guitar and a bass is quite phenomenal. They are talented, professional and entertaining, and the dinner show here is an excellent value.
Bishop Museum, 1525 Bernice Street, Honolulu, Oahu. Tel: (808) 847–3511.

Don Ho

Don Ho is an institution in Waikiki, and it's been said that he's built his career giving open-mouthed kisses to blue-rinsed ladies. His audience seems to love him, and he has an army of devoted fans.
Waikiki Beachcomber Hotel, 2300
Kalakaua Avenue, Waikiki, Honolulu. Tel: (808) 931–3009).

Magic of Polynesia

This is one of the more lavish shows in town, with the illusions of John Hirokawa added to the song and dance.
Hilton Hawaiian Village Dome, 2005 Kalia Road, Honolulu, Oahu. Tel: (808) 949–4321.

Society of Seven

This seven-piece band receives standing ovations for mimicking performers ranging from James Brown to Tina Turner, though it's sometimes hard to tell which is which. If your idea of a great night out is watching men in coconut-stuffed dresses make fools of themselves, then this could be the show for you.
Outrigger Waikiki Hotel, 2335 Kalakaua Avenue, Honolulu, Oahu. Tel: (808) 923–0711.

COMEDY CLUBS
Honolulu Comedy Club

One of the few establishments of its kind in the Islands. Local talent is featured during the week and national headliners at weekends.
Ilikai Hotel, 1777 Ala Moana Boulevard, Honolulu, Oahu. Tel: (808) 949–3811.

Kona Surf Hotel's Comedy Club

Keauhou-Kona, Hawaii. Tel: (808) 332–3411.

CINEMAS

Cinemas showing major first-run films can be found throughout the state, even on little Lanai. In Honolulu there is also the Hawaii IMAX Theater showing a breathtaking film of the Islands on a five-story screen that's 70 feet wide.
325 Seaside Avenue, Honolulu, Oahu.
Tel: (808) 923-4629.

THEATERS

Although theatre does not have a strong tradition in Hawaii, there are a few venues that are worth looking at.

Diamond Head Theater
520 Makapuu Avenue, Honolulu, Oahu.
Tel: (808) 734-0274.

Hawaii Performing Arts Company
Manoa Valley Theater, 2833 East Manoa Valley Road, Honolulu, Oahu. Tel: (808) 521-3487.

Kennedy Theater
Known for outstanding Asian productions.
East-West Center, University of Hawaii, Manoa Campus, Honolulu, Oahu.
Tel: (808) 948-7655.

Neal S. Blaisdell Center
Touring productions of major Broadway shows (see page 48).
777 Ward Avenue, Honolulu, Oahu.
Tel: (808) 521-2911.

CLASSICAL MUSIC
Chamber Music Hawaii
Between October and May the ensembles play at different locations throughout Honolulu.
Tel: (808) 947-1975.

Hawaii Opera Theater
Their winter program is performed at the Neal S. Blaisdell Concert Hall.
Tel: (808) 596-7372.

Honolulu Symphony Orchestra
From September to May the orchestra performs at the Neal S. Blaisdell Concert Hall. During the summer it sponsors an outdoor series at the Waikiki Shell in Kapiolani Park.
Neal S. Blaisdell Concert Hall, 777 Ward Avenue, Honolulu, Oahu. Tel: (808) 593-9291.

The Honolulu Symphony strings at full tilt

HAWAIIAN MUSIC

Banyan Court
*Sheraton Moana Surfrider, 2365
Kalakaua Avenue, Honolulu, Oahu.
Tel: (808) 922–3111.*

House Without a Key
Every evening at cocktail hour, Hawaiian
musicians perform in this idyllic setting as
the sun sets over the Pacific.
*Halekulani Hotel, 2199 Kalia Road,
Honolulu, Oahu. Tel: (808) 923–2311.*

Mai Tai Bar
*Royal Hawaiian Hotel, 2259 Kalakaua
Avenue, Honolulu, Oahu. Tel: (808)
923–7311.*

ROCK

Jazz Cellar
In spite of its name this is the home of
loud rock and roll.
*205 Lewers Street, Honolulu, Oahu.
Tel: (808) 923–9952.*

Moose McGillycuddy's
Live music, dancing and wall-to-wall
people are the trademark.
*310 Lewers Street, Honolulu, Oahu.
Tel: (808) 923–0751.*

Wave Waikiki
This is the leader in progressive bands.
*1877 Kalakaua Avenue, Honolulu, Oahu.
Tel: (808) 941–0424.*

JAZZ

Café Picasso
Jazz singer Jimmy Borges stars here every
weekend.
*Alana Waikiki Hotel, 1956 Ala Moana
Boulevard, Honolulu, Oahu. Tel: (808)
941–7275.*

Captain's Room
*Hawaii Prince Hotel, 100 Holomoana Street,
Honolulu, Oahu. Tel: (808) 956–1111.*

Blackie's Bar
*Honoapiilani Highway, Lahaina, Maui.
Tel: (808) 667–7979.*

Bernstein's *Candide*, Hawaii Opera Theater

NIGHTCLUBS

Annabelle's
*Ilikai Hotel, 1777 Ala Moana Boulevard,
Honolulu, Oahu. Tel: (808) 949–3811.*

Esprit Nightclub
*Sheraton Waikiki Hotel, 2255 Kalakaua
Avenue, Honolulu, Oahu. Tel: (808)
922–4422.*

Maharaja
*Waikiki Trade Center, Seaside at 2255
Kuhio Avenue, Honolulu, Oahu.
Tel: (808) 922–3030.*

Moose McGillycuddy's
*844 Front Street, Lahaina, Maui.
Tel: (808) 667–7758.*

The Point After
*Hawaiian Regent Hotel, 2552 Kalakaua
Avenue, Honolulu, Oahu. Tel: (808)
922–6611.*

Spats
*Hyatt Regency Waikiki, 2424 Kalakaua
Avenue, Honolulu, Oahu. Tel: (808)
923–1234.*

In addition to the usual nightclub scene,
throughout the Islands there are
numerous bars with music and a growing
number of *karaoke* bars, reflecting the
strong Japanese presence in Hawaii.

HULA

According to legend, the first *hula* was performed by Laka, the goddess of dance, to entertain her sister, Pele, the goddess of fire. Pele, delighted with the dance, lit up the sky with fire, and the *hula* became established as a religious dance to honor the gods. Nathaniel Emerson called *hula* "the door to the heart of the people."

Although the dance involves total body movement, it is the hands that tell the story. It was thought that acting out an action in dance would enable that action to be controlled in the future. Dances were performed for wished-for events such as fertility and successful fishing trips.

Both men and women danced the *hula*, the men in loincloths and the women topless. Needless to say, the first missionaries who arrived in the Islands were horrified by this meagre attire, and the sexually suggestive hip gyrations compounded their disgust. The *hula* was immediately banned.

The dance, however, continued in secret, and when

The Kodak Hula Show at Waikiki, Oahu, presents Hawaii's traditional music and movement to appreciative audiences (top, center and right); another display in the luxuriant setting of Waimea Falls Park, Oahu (left)

King Kalakaua came to power in 1874, he revived the tradition – although he required that women cover their upper bodies and wear long skirts.

Predictably, tourism again changed the face of the dance. *Hula kahiko*, the ancient *hula* that was always a purely religious dance, bccame transformed into the grass-skirted, ukulele-playing entertainment that most people now associate with Hawaii. *Hula auwana*, or modern *hula*, was here to stay.

Recently, with the growing interest in Hawaiian roots, there has been a revival of *hula kahiko*. The ancient dance is taught in schools throughout the Islands, *hula* masters are held in high esteem, and *hula* schools compete fiercely to outdo each other. Every April on the Big Island, Hilo's Merrie Monarch Festival is held in honor of King Kalakaua, attracting the best dancers in the state. Tickets sell out several months in advance for this Olympiad of *hula*.

Festivals and Events

JANUARY
Maui
No Mele O Maui.
Oahu
Narcissus Festival, Chinatown, Honolulu.
State Legislature Opening, Honolulu.
Pipeline Bodysurfing Classic, North Shore.

FEBRUARY
Big Island
Mauna Kea Ski Meet.
Oahu
Sandcastle-Building Contest, Kailua Beach Park, Honolulu.
Cherry Blossom Festival, Honolulu.
Hawaiian Open Golf Tournament.
Great Aloha Fun Walk.

MARCH
Big Island
Kona Stampede, Honaunau.
Kauai
Prince Kuhio Ironman/Ironwoman Canoe Race.
Prince Kuhio Day.
Oahu
Hawaiian Song Festival and Song Composing Contest.

APRIL
All Islands
Buddha Day.
Big Island
Merrie Monarch Festival, Hilo (see box).

MAY
Big Island
Honokaa Rodeo.
Oahu
Lei Day, Kapiolani Park, Honolulu.

JUNE
All Islands
King Kamehameha Day (see box).
Oahu
Festival of the Pacific, Honolulu.
Around-the-Island Canoe Race.
Hawaiian Bodysurfing Championships, Point Panic.
King Kamehameha Hula Competition.

JULY
Big Island
Hilo Orchid Society Flower Show, Hilo.
Maui
Makawao Rodeo, Makawao.
Oahu
Annual Ukulele Festival, Kapiolani Park, Honolulu.

AUGUST
Big Island
Macadamia Nut Harvest Festival, Honokaa.
Hawaiian International Billfish Tournament, Kailua-Kona.
Oahu
Hula Festival, Kapiolani Park, Honolulu.
Hawaii State Surfing Championships.
Queen Liliuokalani Keiki Hula Festival.

SEPTEMBER
Big Island
Queen Liliuokalani Canoe Regatta.
Hawaii County Fair, Hilo.
Oahu
Aloha Week (see box).

OCTOBER
Big Island
Ironman Triathlon (see box).
Maui
Maui County Fair.

Aloha Week sees grass-skirted dancers at the opening ceremonies at the Royal Court, Iolani Palace

Molokai
Molokai to Oahu Canoe Race.
Oahu
Honolulu Orchid Society Show,
Honolulu.

NOVEMBER
Big Island
Kona Coffee Cultural Festival, Kailua-
Kona.
Bull and Horse Show, Waimea.

DECEMBER
All Islands
Bodhi Day, Buddhist temples.
Oahu
Honolulu Marathon.
Festival of Trees.
Hawaiian Pro Surfing Championships.
Pipeline Masters, Men's and Women's
World Cup.
Mission Houses Museum Candlelight
Tour.

BEST FESTIVALS
The **Merrie Monarch Festival** in Hilo
is the state's most traditional and
famous *hula* contest, named in honor
of King Kalakaua. It's so popular that
tickets are sold by lottery.

King Kamehameha Day, on 11
June, is a state holiday with festivities
on every island. In Honolulu there is a
lei-draping ceremony at the
Kamehameha statue.

Aloha Week is celebrated on all the
islands with parades, *luaus*, historical
pageants and all kinds of
entertainment.

The **Ironman Triathlon** attracts a
surprisingly large number of people
who want to swim 2.4 miles, followed
by a 112-mile bike ride and then a full
marathon. Definitely more fun to
watch than do!

Children

*H*awaii is a paradise for all ages, and parents can relax knowing that their children are welcomed and catered to. Virtually all car rental companies provide car seats, which are mandatory for children weighing under 40 pounds.

Angst-free flights
There's no getting round the boredom factor inherent in a minimum five-hour flight across the Pacific. Have crayons, games, books, chewing gum (to ease pressure pain in the ears) and other diversions ready during the flight to start the holiday off on the right foot, with everyone keeping their sanity. Most North American airlines cater to children of all ages and provide appropriate meals for them.

At your hotel
Hotels usually provide cribs and roll-away beds at little or no extra cost, but

Swimming with dolphins, Hilton Waikoloa

always phone ahead to make sure your requirements are in place before you arrive.

The bigger resort hotels offer *keiki* programs throughout the day for children aged five and above. Trained staff keep the kids busy with all kinds of activities from *lei*-making and *hula* lessons to building sand castles. Such programs can make a big difference to the parents' enjoyment, so check this out before booking.

The major hotels also offer safe, reliable baby-sitting services. Two bonded private services are **Aloha Babysitting Services** on Oahu (tel: 808 732–2029) and **Babysitting Services** on Maui (tel: 808 661–0558).

Fun times

All the islands offer plenty of outdoor activities, but for the greatest variety of diversions Oahu comes out on top. **Sea Life Park** (see page 56) has fascinating underwater viewing tanks and impressive shows in their two outdoor theaters. In Honolulu, the **Waikiki Aquarium** (see page 50) has a touching pool and also offers guided reef walks. The **Hawaiian Humane Society** has a bird park complete with a turtle pond in a quiet wooded corner of Honolulu. Just past Diamond Head, dolphins are fed at the **Kahala Hilton Hotel** every day at 11am, 2pm and 4pm.

The **Bishop Museum** (page 34) has hands-on exhibits in the Castle Memorial Building. In 1996, the new **Children's Discovery Center** opens at the **Kakaako Waterfront Park** and promises to be an outstanding experience. The children's playground on the *mauka* side of **Kapiolani Park** has swings and other adventure play equipment. For older children the **Ice Palace** near Pearl City is a fun contrast to splashing around in 80°F water. Out of Honolulu, both **Waimea Falls Park** (page 57) and the **Polynesian Cultural Center** (page 54) never fail to keep kids entertained, and the **Dole Plantation** (page 53) offers pony rides into the pineapple fields.

Four Seasons Resort, Wailea, Maui

Sensible swimming

Good beaches abound on every island, but the greatest caution should be taken with swimming in the ocean. On many beaches there are extremely dangerous undercurrents. On Kauai, Wailua's lovely **Lydgate Park** has two large lava pools that are perfect for children, but in general it is safer to stick to hotel pools.

Health concerns

There are excellent medical facilities on all the islands; they are listed under "Hospitals" in the Yellow Pages. In Honolulu, **Kapiolani Medical Center for Women and Children** at 1319 Punahou Street (tel: 808 973–8511) can be contacted in case of emergency. There is also a **Poison Control Center** (tel: 941–4411 in Oahu) or 1–800/362–3585 from the outer islands (toll-free).

Hawaiian Humane Society Bird Park, 2700 Waianae Avenue, Honolulu, Oahu. Tel: (808) 946–2187.
Ice Palace, 4510 Salt Lake Boulevard, Honolulu, Oahu. Tel: (808) 487–9921.
Kahala Hilton Hotel, 5000 Kahala Avenue, Honolulu, Oahu. Tel: (808) 734–2211.

Sports

Spectator sports have never had a strong following in Hawaii, but the main venue for indoor events is the Neal S. Blaisdell Center (see page 48). The state has no teams of any national importance. The only major event for team sports is the Hula Bowl, an American football game played between eastern and western college teams in the Aloha Stadium in January.

Participant sports are a different matter, however, and in fact are one of the main reasons for visiting the Islands. Golf is the number one attraction. Several of the world's most beautiful and most challenging golf courses can be found here, and many visitors never leave their golf resort. Tennis has a smaller but no less enthusiastic following, and many retirees from the pro circuit are coaching on Hawaiian tennis ranches. Water sports inevitably have a high profile. Surfing started here in Hawaii and continues to flourish among younger visitors, and windsurfing now has equal prominence. Sailing, deep-sea fishing, skin diving, sub-aqua diving and kayaking are also popular.

GOLF

Each island has a golf course for every level of ability and for every pocket. All the major course designers have examples of their work on at least one of the islands, and many of their courses here are considered to be among the world's best, in terms of both beauty and technical challenge.

Oahu

The Arnold Palmer-designed course at the **Turtle Bay Hilton** (tel: 808 293–8574) and the **Sheraton Makaha West Golf Course** (tel: 808 695–9544) are ranked among the best. In Honolulu the **Ala Wai Golf Course** (tel: 808 296–4653) and the **Hawaii Kai Golf Course** (tel: 808 395–2358) are popular

with visitors and locals alike. The cheapest round of golf on the Islands is at the **Bay View Golf Club** (tel: 808 247–0451).

Kauai

Kauai has three outstanding and spectacular courses at **Princeville** on the North Shore (tel: 808 826–3580). Robert Trent Jones designed one of the courses here, and Jack Nicklaus designed the Kiele Course as well as the Kauai Lagoons Course at the **Kauai Lagoon Golf Club** (tel: 808 241–6000) near Lihue. In Poipu is the 18-hole **Poipu Bay Resort Golf Course** (tel: 808 742–8711). For the budget golfer, the **Wailua Municipal Golf Course** (tel: 808 241–6666) may not be the most visually appealing, but it is certainly the cheapest.

The course on the coast at Poipu, Kauai, lets players soak up the island's jewel-like setting

Maui

Maui has several courses, both public and private. The **Royal Kaanapali Golf Courses** (tel: 808 661–3691) were designed by Robert Trent Jones Sr. and are among the island's best. Arnold Palmer designed the ocean-front Bay Course, one of three courses at the **Kapalua Resort Golf Club** (tel: 808 669–8044). A third course, by Robert Trent Jones Jr., has recently been added at the **Wailea Golf Club** (tel: 808 879–2966), and the **Makena Golf Course** (tel: 808 879–3344) offers beautiful views to neighboring islands. **Waiehu Municipal Golf Course** (tel: 808 243–7400) offers the best value on Maui.

Big Island

The Big Island is a golfer's heaven. Some of the very best courses in the US are to be found here, mainly along the South Kohala Coast, which boasts six championship courses. The **Mauna Kea Beach Golf Course** (tel: 808 882–5888) is one of the most challenging, and next door to it is the new **Hapuna Golf Course** (tel: 808 882–1035) designed by Arnold Palmer. Further down the coast are two 18-hole courses at **Mauna Lani Resort Golf Course** (tel: 808 885–6655). The best bargains are on the Hilo side of the island, with unbelievably low green fees. However, the weather here is far less reliable. **Hilo Municipal Golf Course** (tel: 808 959–7711) is very popular, and reservations are recommended for weekends. The **Volcano Golf and Country Club** (tel: 808 967–7331) offers the unique experience of providing an active volcano as a hazard.

Lanai and Molokai

Both Lanai and Molokai have courses. On Lanai, **The Experience** at Koele (tel: 808 565–4653) was designed by Greg Norman, and the **Cavendish Golf Course** (tel: 808 565–7233) is an inexpensive 9-hole course in Lanai City. **Ironwood Hills** (tel: 808 567–6000) and **Kaluakoi** (tel: 808 552–2739) are the only courses on Molokai.

TENNIS

On Oahu alone there are over 168 county-maintained tennis courts, plus private and hotel courts that are open to the public. Some of the major resort hotels have resident pros available for coaching. For information on municipal courts, contact the Department of Parks and Recreation:

Big Island: 25 Aupuni Street, Hilo. Tel: (808) 961–8311. Kauai: PO Box 111, Lihue. Tel: (808) 245–4751. Maui: 200 High Street, Wailuku. Tel: (808) 244–7750. Oahu: Tennis Division, 3908 Paki Avenue, Honolulu. Tel: (808) 923–7927.

HORSEBACK RIDING

Riding is popular throughout the Islands. Most stables offer trail rides lasting from one hour to all day, for all levels of experience.

Kauai: CJM Country Stables, Poipu, tel: (808) 742–6096. Pooku Stables, Princeville, tel: (808) 826–6777.
Maui: Adventures on Horseback, Haleakala, tel: (808) 242–7445.

Charlie's Trail Rides and Pack Trips, tel: (808) 248–8209. Ironwood Ranch, West Maui, tel: (808) 669–4991. Pony Express Tours, tel: (808) 667–2200. Thompson Ranch and Riding Stables, tel: (808) 878–1910.
Oahu: Kualoa Ranch, Windward Coast, tel: (808) 237–8515. Turtle Bay Hilton, North Shore, tel: (808) 293–8811.
Big Island: Kohala Trail Riding, Kohala, tel: (808) 889–6257. Mauna Kea Stables, Waimea, tel: (808) 885–4288. Paniolo Riding Adventures, tel: (808) 889–5354.

BICYCLING

Hawaii has very few biking trails and, as most of the islands are mountainous, the going can be tough. A popular diversion is to "van-pool" to a high point and cruise down (see page 137).

Bicycle rental is available on all the islands, and is listed in the Yellow Pages.

WATER SPORTS

To visit Hawaii without getting wet is to miss half the fun of the islands. Throughout Hawaii there are companies offering everything from deep-sea fishing to scuba (sub-aqua) lessons – basically, if it happens in water, then someone rents out equipment or gives lessons. The Yellow Pages list suppliers under their appropriate headings.

Windsurfing

This now rivals surfing in popularity. The best place for beginners is **Anini Beach** on Kauai's North Shore, where the breezes are gentle and warm. For both beginners and intermediates, Oahu's **Lanikai Beach** on Kailua Bay is a good spot, and for the advanced windsurfer there is nothing to beat **Hookipa Beach** on Maui.

Kayaking

The ultimate kayak trips – but only for the most experienced – are off the Na Pali Coast of Kauai and the Windward Coast of Molokai, both set against dramatic sea cliffs. But even during the summer, huge waves can make these locations a serious

undertaking. For beginners, both Kailua Bay on Oahu's Windward Shore and the Huleia Stream near Lihue on Kauai are ideal training grounds. For equipment rental contact the following:

On the Big Island: Kona Kai-Yak, Kailua-Kona, tel: (808) 326–2922. On Kauai: Kauai by Kayak, Lihue, tel: (808) 245–9662. On Maui: Ocean Kayaking, Kihei, tel: (808) 874–6330. On Oahu: Two Good Kayak Hawaii, tel: (808) 262– 5656.

Snorkelling and scuba diving

Clear blue waters and brightly hued fish make Hawaii an excellent destination for exploring the depths, and its reefs are a great place for learning. Most of the major hotels offer lessons; some rent equipment. All dive shops have maps and can advise on current conditions.

The premier diving site is **Molokini Crater Marine Preserve** off Maui, and there are several companies offering boat trips there as well as to other offshore diving areas. Most of the boats leave

Maalaea Harbor on Maui, but the catamaran *Kai Nani* leaves from the Maui Prince Hotel and gets a half-hour start on all the other boats (tel: 808 874–1111). The following are among the best diving locations in the islands:

On the Big Island: Kealakekua Bay, Kahaluu Beach Park, Napoopoo Beach Park, Old Airport Beach, Hapuna Beach State Park. On Kauai: Haena Beach, Moloaa and Koloa Landing. On Maui: Honolua Bay, Baldwin Beach Park and Waianapanapa State Park. On Oahu: Hanauma Bay and Kahe Point.

Hawaiians have been jumping onto their boards and riding the waves for at least 600 years. Legends and chants dating back to the 14th century mention the sport, and in 1778 one of Captain Cook's officers seemed impressed with their prowess when he wrote: "The boldness and address, with which we saw them perform these difficult and dangerous manoeuvres, was altogether astonishing and is scarce to be credited."

It seemed that everyone who went to Hawaii was amazed by this daring pastime. Mark Twain visited the Islands in 1866 and commented: "It did not seem that a lightning express train could shoot along at a more hair-lifting speed."

The Hawaiian wave riders of yesteryear were as fanatical about their sport as today's surf bums. If the surf looked good, nothing else mattered. Work stopped, wives took second place, and riding the waves took over. The advent of the missionaries discouraged this decadent pursuit, and by the beginning of this century much of the tradition had been lost.

Its resurgence is often credited to Jack London, who wrote *A Royal Sport:*

SURF'S UP!

Surfing sets the classic contest of man against nature – and man often takes a tumble!

Surfing at Waikiki, in 1907. This flowery piece glamorized the sport with such hero-worshipping lines as: "… not struggling frantically in that wild movement, not buried and crushed and buffeted by those mighty monsters, but standing above them all, calm and superb, poised on the giddy summit, his feet buried in the churning foam, the salt smoke rising to his knees …"

Tourism consolidated the interest, and in 1908 the Outrigger Canoe Club was formed on land at Waikiki. In the following years the sport gained an increasingly wide following, spreading to California and Australia and ultimately to wherever the surf can rise to the occasion.

The sport has come a long way since the days of 10-foot-long wooden boards. Modern surfboards are space-age laminates designed to get the most out of every kind of wave that comes along.

Food and Drink

*H*awaii has not had a tradition of fine food. Polynesian cuisine is a taste acquired from birth, and not for nothing have Polynesian restaurants failed to fire the imagination of the world's gourmets. A visit to a *luau* will be as close as most tourists will want to get to an authentic meal.

At the Makai Market, Ala Moana Center, you can sample fast food of many cultures

Until recently, some of the best food was from small ethnic restaurants of many of the immigrant groups to the Islands, such as the Chinese, Filipinos and, more recently, Vietnamese. But there has been a dramatic change. Major hotels and resorts started to attract talented chefs from Europe and the mainland who were not satisfied with producing run-of-the-mill hotel restaurant fare. They demanded Hawaii's freshest produce and drew on the diverse ethnic cuisines already in existence, developing a distinctive cuisine that has raised the level of dining in Hawaii to that of New York and San Francisco. In comparison with the mainland, however, meals in Hawaii are very expensive.

The group of innovators call their creation Hawaiian Regional Cuisine (HRC). Their restaurants can be found throughout the Islands, both in hotels and as independent establishments. While membership of the HRC group will not guarantee great food, it will always be at least interesting. Their presence has had the added bonus of spurring on other restaurants to better their offerings.

Fast food
Fast-food chains abound – McDonalds, Burger King, Wendy's, Kentucky Fried Chicken and Pizza Hut dominate the market in the Islands just as they do on the mainland. Any one will provide very cheap, predictable food in hygienic surroundings.

Casual dining
One step above fast food are coffee shops. You'll find the usual chains, such as Howard Johnson's and Denny's. While they serve perfectly edible food, it will never be memorable. As on the mainland, most are open 24 hours and offer children's menus.

For something less generic, you might try these casual restaurants. Oahu: Waiahole Poi Factory, Friday afternoons, Kamehameh Highway and Waiahole Valley Road. The Big Island: Kona Ranch House, Kuakini and Palani highways. Kauai: Aloha Diner, 971 F Kuhio Highway. Maui: Lahaina Broiler, 889 Front Street.

Price range per person for a three-course meal (excluding beverages, tax and tip):
$ under $10
$$ under $25
$$$ under $40
$$$$ over $40

OAHU

Bali-by-the-Sea $$$$
Elegant dining with spectacular views.
Hilton Hawaiian Village, 2005 Kalia Road, Honolulu. Tel: (808) 949–4321.

Jameson's by the Sea $$
Wonderful views over the North Shore, with great seafood.
62–540 Kamehameha Highway, Haleiwa. Tel: (808) 637–4336.

Keo's Thai Cuisine $$
Deservedly the most popular gourmet Thai cuisine in the Islands.
625 Kapahulu Avenue, Waikiki. Tel: (808) 737–8240.

La Mer $$$$
One of the great restaurants of Hawaii, thanks to chef George Mavrothalassitis.
Halekulani Hotel, 2199 Kalia Road, Waikiki. Tel: (808) 923–2311.

Michel's at the Colony Surf $$$$
A Waikiki classic that has been eclipsed by some of the newcomers.
Colony Surf Hotel, 2895 Kalakaua Avenue, Waikiki. Tel: (808) 923–6552.

Restaurant Suntory $$$
Authentic Japanese cuisine with a choice of three styles of restaurant.
Royal Hawaiian Center, 2233 Kalakaua Avenue, Waikiki. Tel: (808) 922–5511.

Roy's Restaurant $$$$
Roy Yamaguchi established Hawaiian Regional Cuisine at this remarkable restaurant, and it's well worth the long drive out of Honolulu.
Hawaii Kai Corporate Plaza, 6600 Kalanianaole Highway. Tel: (808) 396–7697.

Saigon Café $
Vietnamese food is the best value in town, and this one is a notch above the rest.
1831 Ala Moana Boulevard, Waikiki. Tel: (808) 955–4009.

Sunset Grill $$$
One of the better establishments on Restaurant Row.
500 Ala Moana Boulevard, Honolulu. Tel: (808) 521–4409.

Yummy Korean Bar-B-Q $
Korean barbecues are everywhere and have good, tasty food at incredibly low prices, but don't expect white table linen. This one is particularly good. Makai Market has several good, cheap cafés.
Ala Moana Center, Makai Market, 1450 Ala Moana Boulevard, Honolulu. Tel: (808) 946–9188.

Japanese breakfast, Halekulani Hotel, Waikiki

BIG ISLAND

Canoe House $$$$
The Hawaiian Regional Cuisine of chef Alan Wong.
Mauna Lani Bay Hotel, South Kohala. Tel: (808) 885–6622.

Dining Room at the Ritz Carlton $$$$
Elegant dining under the creative control of Chef Amy Ferguson-Ota.
Ritz-Carlton Hotel, Mauna Lani Bay, South Kohala. Tel: (808) 885–2000.

Merriman's $$$$
Peter Merriman is another talented interpreter of HRC.
Opelo Plaza, Route 19, Waimea. Tel: (808) 885–6822.

Tom Bombadil's Food and Drink $
Pizza and casual dining with great ocean views.
75-5864 Walua Road, Kailua-Kona. Tel: (808) 329–1292.

KAUAI

A Pacific Café $$$$
One of America's finest restaurants. In an unlikely location, Jean-Marie Josselin blends the best of the Islands with a traditional French foundation.
Kauai Village Shopping Center, Kapaa. Tel: (808) 822–0013.

West of the Moon Café $
Best breakfasts on the island.
Kauhale Center, Kuhio Highway and Aku Road. Tel: (808) 826–7640.

LANAI

The Lodge at Koele Dining Room $$$$
Superb dining, elegant surroundings.
Lodge at Koele, Lanai City. Tel: (808) 565–7300.

MAUI

Avalon $$$
Chef Mark Ellerman's Hawaiian Regional Cuisine can be very good, but isn't consistent.
844 Front Street, Lahaina. Tel: (808) 667–5559.

David Paul's Lahaina Grill $$$
Creative East-West cuisine.
127 Lahainaluna Road, Lahaina. Tel: (808) 667–5117.

Gerard's $$$$
Outstanding French nouvelle cuisine in a comfortable country inn ambience.
174 Lahainaluna Road, Lahaina. Tel: (808) 661–8939.

Hailiimaile General Store $$$
Bev and Joe Gannon were in the music business before they converted this up-

EATING LOCAL STYLE

Anyone venturing outside a hotel to eat will inevitably come across local dishes. A few are Polynesian, but many come from Hawaii's numerous ethnic groups.

Adobo – a Filipino dish of stewed chicken

Ahi – yellowfin tuna

A'u – marlin

Char siu – Chinese roast pork

Chicken long rice – transparent noodles with shredded chicken

Crack seed – dried, sweetened tropical fruit and seeds

Haupia – custard of thickened coconut milk

Kalua pork – the centerpiece of every *luau*. A whole pig is baked in an *imu* (underground pit), becoming very tender, with a smoky taste

Kimchee – Korean fermented cabbage with chillies – keep the water handy!

Laulau – pork, *taro* leaves and butterfish steamed in a parcel of *ti* leaves

Lilikoi – passion fruit

Limu – Hawaiian seaweed

Lomi lomi salmon – salted salmon mixed with chopped tomatoes and spring onions, served chilled

Mahimahi – popular fish with firm, moist flesh, sometimes incorrectly termed "dolphin"

Malasadas – Portuguese doughnut holes

Manapua – steamed buns, often containing pork or bean paste

Ono – wahoo, a mackerel considered one of the most delicious fish in the ocean

Plate lunch – these cheap prepacked lunches can include *mahimahi*, teriyaki chicken, *lomi* salmon or *laulau*, plus two scoops of rice and a portion of salad

Pão dolce – a sweetish Portuguese bread

Poi – an unappetizing goo loved by locals: cooked *taro* root pounded into a purple paste

Poki – a seafood salad that includes *limu*

Pu pu – hors-d'oeuvres and finger foods

Saimin – this noodle soup is served almost everywhere, even McDonald's. Variations include adding chicken or beef

Shave ice – finely shaved ice with fruit-flavored syrup poured over it

Tako – octopus

Taro chips – deep-fried slices of *taro* root.

country general store into one of the best restaurants in Hawaii. Hollywood friends often drop in for dinner.
900 Hailiimaile Road, Hailiimaile. Tel: (808) 572-2666.

Longhi's $$$

Popular with the young crowd. Basic Italian with no written menus, the waiters recite everything.
888 Front Street, Lahaina. Tel: (808) 667-2288.

Prince Court $$$$

Home to Roger Dikon's interpretation of Hawaiian Regional Cuisine.
Maui Prince Hotel, 5400 Makena Alanui Road, Makena. Tel: (808) 874-1111.

Sound of the Falls $$$$

Exceptional food, exquisite surroundings.
Westin Maui Hotel, 2365 Kaanapali Parkway, Lahaina. Tel: (808) 667-2525.

LUAUS

The word *luau* means a feast. Wherever there is a *luau*, there is certain to be food in abundance. This is the ultimate Polynesian party – and, unlike Christmas or Thanksgiving, it can be held on any day of the year.

Most *luaus* are now nothing more than commercial enterprises aimed at tourists. Although these bear little resemblance to the original concept, they are always based on tradition, albeit obscure.

Every *luau* serves some dishes that are uniquely Polynesian, and the centerpiece is always *kalua* pig, which requires elaborate preparation. First, a hole in the ground is lined with rocks which are heated with a mesquite wood fire; this underground roasting pit is called an *imu*. When the rocks are hot, a whole pig, wrapped in *ti* and banana leaves, is placed in the *imu*. Other foods, also wrapped in banana leaves, are placed round the pig. The whole thing is covered with more leaves and a layer of earth, which seals in the heat. After four to eight hours the food is cooked.

The opening of the *imu* signals the start of the *luau*. Accompanying dishes usually include *poi*, sweet potato, *lomi lomi* salmon and a coconut dessert called *haupia*. There is also chicken, beef, fish and as many exotic tropical drinks as you can handle.

No *luau* is complete without a Polynesian show, including *hula* girls – and boys – together with a variety of other acts that vary with the *luau*.

The evolution of the *luau*: from native feast to tourist feed at PCC and Germaine's

The *luau* grounds are away from the beach, but the atmosphere leaves little to be desired. The Polynesian show, unfortunately, may not always live up to the rest of the evening.

On Maui, Old Lahaina Luau, on the beach at the southern end of town, is delightful. The food is a happy balance of good traditional dishes and food more acceptable to Western palates. The *luau* grounds overlook the ocean and provide a perfect stage for the setting sun.

On Oahu, Germaine's Luau is held nightly on a beach 35 minutes from Honolulu. Buses provide transportation from major Honolulu hotels. This is a party on a massive scale, with hundreds of participants. Although the *luau* is the least authentic in terms of food or entertainment, it is nevertheless one of the most popular with locals.

Opinions vary on which *luaus* are best, but there are a handful that get unanimously high praise. On the Big Island, the Friday night *luau* at Kona Village is generally considered to serve the most authentic food in the Islands.

Hotels and Accommodations

*H*awaii lives on tourism, and inevitably there is a tremendous range of accommodations on all the main islands. Altogether there are over 65,000 hotel rooms available in the state. However, compared to mainland USA, there are few bargains to be found. Hotel prices are high, and the budget motel simply does not exist here. In its place are several bed-and-breakfast establishments, but these vary greatly in style and price. Nevertheless, almost all of the accommodations are of a universally high standard. Even the cheaper places are clean and very well equipped. At the other end of the scale are hotels that provide the ultimate in luxury, with rooms and service that are acknowledged to be the best in the world.

Sybarite's delight: the seductive pool at the clifftop Princeville Hotel, on Kauai's North Shore

Budget travel

Hostels are in short supply in Hawaii. There is only one official American Youth Hostel, located in Honolulu, and it is always very busy. Two other youth hostels operate in Waikiki. There are more YMCAs, and they accept either men or women. There are five on Oahu, one on Maui and one on Kauai.

Each hostel varies regarding the accommodations it offers, but many have a room with a bath or shower for about $20. Several of the hostels impose a three-day maximum stay.
YMCA Central Branch, 401 Atkinson Drive, Honolulu, HI 96814. Tel: (808) 941–3344.

Bed-and-breakfast

These privately owned properties can

differ greatly from each other, but the price range is usually from $55 to $85 a night. The disadvantage is that ideally they should be booked one to three months in advance through an agency. It is unlikely that you'd find something available on a last-minute impulse, although it is always worth trying. Most B&Bs are listed with several different agencies, so there is little point in contacting too many. Turning up on the doorstep is not always appreciated; however, the agencies listed below all provide a professional service tailored to the needs of the client.

Deluxe, yet with a timeless air of style

The agencies try to match clients with accommodations, which run the gamut from mansions to cottages. They all offer the unique experience of sharing the life of a Hawaiian family. Almost all B&Bs will insist on a three-day minimum stay. The agencies listed below cover bookings on all the islands, with the exception of **My Island**, which is restricted to the Big Island.

All Islands Bed and Breakfast, 823 Kainui Drive, Kailua, Oahu, HI 96734. Tel: (808) 263–2342. Fax: (808) 263–0308.

Bed and Breakfast Hawaii, Box 449, Kapaa, Kauai, HI 96746. Tel: (808) 822–7771. Fax: (808) 822–2723.

My Island Bed and Breakfast, Box 100, Volcano, Big Island, HI 96785. Tel: (808) 967–7216. Fax: (808) 967–7719.

Pacific Hawaii Bed and Breakfast, 19 Kai Nani Place, Kailua, Oahu, HI 96734. Tel: (808) 262–6026. Fax: (808) 261–6573.

Condominiums

Condominiums are privately owned apartments which are most often part of a huge high-rise development. Staying in one is like staying in a self-catering hotel, except that there is usually no maid service and none of the other amenities associated with hotels. Most of the condominiums are in popular resort areas such as Kaanapali on Maui, South Kohala on the Big Island, or Waikiki, which means there are always plenty of restaurants and other services within very easy reach. All linen is provided, but the quality and extent of furnishings is up to the individual owner, and this should be checked on before making a reservation.

Paying for them is no more difficult than for a hotel room, except that deposits are required on booking and cancellation penalties can be quite stiff. There is usually a minimum stay requirement that varies with the season.

Condominiums offer ideal accommodations for a family or group of friends traveling together and provide a relatively inexpensive alternative to resort hotels.

The best listing is in the *Member Accommodation Guide* published by the Hawaii Visitors Bureau. This only lists members of the HVB, but nevertheless it is very comprehensive.

The Royal Hawaiian Hotel, a charming anachronism of low pink curves amidst soulless linear giants

Boutique hotels

Over the past few years, many of the small, run-down hotels in Waikiki have been transformed. Now completely refurbished and converted into exquisite, intimate accommodations, they may not have all the services of the bigger hotels but lack nothing of their luxury. Their rates are very reasonable compared to similar rooms in the deluxe properties.

Alana Waikiki Hotel, 1956 Ala Moana Boulevard, Waikiki. Tel: (808) 941–7275. Fax: (808) 949–0996.

Aston Waikiki Beachside Hotel, 2452 Kalakaua Avenue, Waikiki. Tel: (808) 931–2100. Fax: (808) 922–8785.

Kaulana Kai Hotel, 2425 Kuhio Avenue, Waikiki. Tel: (808) 943–0202. Fax: (808) 922–9473.

Royal Garden Hotel, 440 Olohana Street, Waikiki. Tel: (808) 943–0202. Fax: (808) 946–8777.

Waikiki Joy Hotel, 320 Lewers Street, Waikiki. Tel: (808) 923–2300. Fax: (808) 924–4010.

Classic Hawaii

Tourism is still fairly new to Hawaii, so there are very few old classic hotels on the Islands, but a handful of historic properties are worth considering.

On Hawaii, **Kilauea Lodge** (PO Box 116, Volcano, HI 96785. Tel: 808 967–7366) is a delightfully converted YMCA with strong historic ties. Close by is the famous **Volcano House** (PO Box 53, Hawaii Volcanoes National Park, HI 96718. Tel: 808 967–7321), actually on the edge of the Kilauea crater. On Maui, the **Pioneer Inn** (658 Wharf Street, Lahaina, HI 96761. Tel: 808 661–3636) captures the romance of old whaling times, when the bar downstairs would be jammed with sailors. In Waikiki, the **Royal Hawaiian Hotel** (2255 Kalakaua Avenue, Honolulu, HI 96815. Tel: 808 923–7311) is now surrounded by modern high-rises, but the Pink Palace, as it is known, is still a Waikiki landmark (see page 62).

Staying in style

Those searching for pure, unadulterated luxury will find the choice is bewildering. These are the very best:

Big Island: Mauna Lani Bay Hotel and Bungalows; Ritz-Carlton Mauna Lani.
Kauai: Hyatt Regency Kauai; Princeville Hotel.
Lanai: The Lodge at Koele; Manele Bay Hotel.
Maui: Four Seasons Resort; Grand Wailea Resort; Hotel Hana Kai-Maui; Ritz-Carlton Kapalua.
Oahu: Halekulani Hotel, Waikiki; Sheraton Moana Surfrider, Waikiki; Hyatt Regency Waikiki.

The bungalows at the **Mauna Lani Bay Hotel** come with their own butler and maid for a mere $2,500 a night!

The biggest impact on the luxury market was made by developer Chris Hemmeter, whose monumental resorts took extravagance to new heights. The **Hilton Waikoloa** on the Big Island extends over 62 acres and you are transported to your room either by boat or monorail. You can swim with dolphins or stroll the mile-long museum walkway. His **Kauai Lagoons** development, a neo-Roman fantasy, suffered extreme damage in Hurricane Iniki and has been taken over by Marriott Hotels. On Maui, the **Westin Maui** is one of his more tasteful and restrained properties, with just enough glitter to make it stand out from the crowd.

On a more modest note, two Hawaiian groups of hotels offer a wide range of accommodations at reasonable prices: **Aston Hotels and Resorts** (tel: 808 931–1400) and **Outrigger Hotels** (tel: 303 369–7777).

Kaluakoi Hotel and Golf Club

GETTING THE BEST VALUE

Tremendous value can be found in package deals from the mainland. These include airfare, hotel and car rental at prices below the cost of an ordinary return airfare. A good travel agent should have access to these packages.

When making reservations for any accommodation, make sure the location is convenient. Ask plenty of questions. It is also worth asking if there are any special rates available. Many places will give a significant discount rather than lose your business, so it never does any harm to ask.

Many hotels do not charge for local calls, but long-distance calls from in-room telephones can be marked up outrageously, and there is often a charge for reverse-charge or credit-card calls. Always find out what these charges are to avoid a nasty shock at bill-paying time. All hotels have public telephones available in lobby areas, and they can be far less expensive.

The enticing contents of mini-bars in hotel rooms always cost far more than you expect. Often the hotel gift shop has the same items for a fraction of the price.

On Business

*W*hether it is fortunate or unfortunate to be in Hawaii on business is debateable! The business world is certainly more relaxed in Hawaii, and formal suits and ties are the exception. Business practices are the same as on the mainland or in Europe. In fact, the business world has become so uniform it can be hard to distinguish one place from another.

The general visa and immigration rules (see page 176) apply to foreign business travelers intending to leave the country within a 6-month period. Special visas are necessary for extended stays and for permission to work in the US; get advice from the closest American Consulate.

Honolulu is the only international business center in the state, and is also a center for Pacific Rim countries. The main engine of the economy is tourism, followed closely by the military. Together they represent over 60 percent of the state's income. The rest comes from agriculture (sugar, pineapples and macadamia nuts), construction and manufacturing.

ACCOMMODATIONS

Major hotels have good facilities for business travelers, including business centres with full secretarial services. Meeting rooms are often available. In Waikiki several of the small boutique hotels cater specifically to the business traveler. On islands other than Oahu, the major resort hotels usually have full conference facilities.

BANKS

Few European banks are represented in Honolulu. There are, however, numerous American banks for local currency transactions. Any of the Thomas Cook locations listed on page 185 can transmit funds to or from

overseas, by telegraphic transfer. Any bank will also be able to accept funds wired from overseas. Funds wired in US dollars reduce delays and bank charges. Banking hours are generally Monday to Thursday 8:30am–3pm, Friday till 6pm.

BUSINESS HOURS

Most offices are open Monday to Friday from 8:30am to 5pm, but longer hours and weekend hours are common. Most business support services close over weekends. Post offices are open Monday to Friday from 8 or 8:30am to 4:30 or 5pm and from 8am to noon on Saturdays.

BUSINESS MEDIA

The Honolulu Advertiser, the biggest daily newspaper, carries items of local business news. Monthly magazines of interest to business travelers include *Hawaii Business, Pacific Business News, Hawaii Hospitality* and *Hawaii Investor*.

TV/Radio

CNN – cable television channel giving regular business and stock market news throughout the day.
KHVH-AM 990 – all-news ABC and NBC affiliate.
KHPR-FM 88.1 – public broadcasting station carrying BBC World Service News.
KKUA-FM 90.7 – public broadcasting station, as above.

COMMUNICATIONS

The telephone system is excellent, with direct dialing to over 70 countries, and there are rarely problems with either fax transmission or the use of computer modems. For local directory assistance dial 1–411; for the mainland dial 1 + area code + 555–1212. International directory inquiries are available through the operator.

The majority of hotels have a fax machine available. Some of the bigger hotels provide modem sockets in the rooms.

CONFERENCE AND EXHIBITION SITES

Neal S. Blaisdell Center, 777 Ward Avenue, Honolulu. Tel: (808) 527–5400; fax: (808) 527–5499.
Dole Ballrooms, 735 Iwilei Road, Honolulu. Tel: (808) 531–3127; fax: (808) 531–4819.
Hawaii Imin International Conference Center, 1777 East-West Road, Honolulu. Tel: (808) 944–7159; fax: (808) 944–7170.
Hawaii Maritime Center/Pier 7, Pier 7, Honolulu. Tel: (808) 523–6151; fax: (808) 538–1519.

INTERNATIONAL COURIER SERVICES

DHL Worldwide Express, tel: (1–800) 225–5345; **Federal Express**, tel: (1–800) 238–5355; **United States Postal Service**, tel: (1–800) 222–1811 (all toll-free).

SECRETARIAL SERVICES

Secretarial help is listed in the Yellow Pages.

TRANSLATION SERVICES

Academia Language School, tel: (808) 946–5599; **Ace Translations and Services Inc**, tel: (808) 591–2334; **Asian Research Center**, tel: (808) 949–4822; **AT Translators**, tel: (1–800) 443–2444 (toll-free).

TRANSPORT

Hawaiian Airlines, Aloha Airlines and Island Air all provide a fast, efficient service between islands. Private aircraft and helicopters are available for charter and are listed at length in the Yellow Pages, as are limousine services.

Honolulu's downtown financial district gleams with bullish confidence

Practical Guide

FOR VISITORS FROM OVERSEAS

ARRIVING
Entry requirements

Travelers from Australia and South Africa need a visa. Travelers from the UK, New Zealand and Canada do not require a visa for stays up to 90 days or less, but are asked to complete a visa waiver form by their airline or shipping company. All travelers must carry a passport (valid for at least six months except in the case of UK passport holders) and a ticket for return or onward travel from the USA.

Travelers who require visas should obtain them in their country of residence, as it may prove difficult to obtain them elsewhere. In the UK, the Thomas Cook Passport and Visa Service can advise on and obtain the necessary documentation – consult your Thomas Cook travel consultant. While in the USA, visitors can take a side-trip overland or by sea into Canada or Mexico and re-enter without a visa, within their overall 90-day stay.

Immigration laws are both complicated and strictly enforced, and it is advisable to check with the American Consulate well before departure.

By air

Honolulu International is the main airport for international flights into Hawaii, handling several American and international airlines. Flights from the West Coast of America also use Maui's Kahului Airport and Kona's Keahole Airport on the Big Island.

The only scheduled flights allowed to terminate in Honolulu are with the North American domestic carriers.

Honolulu International Airport has

two terminals, one international and one inter-island. A free bus service called the *wiki wiki* runs between them. The main terminal is a vast complex of shops and restaurants, and many of the gates are a considerable distance from the check-in area. Both terminals cater to disabled travelers.

Flights between islands are frequent. In addition to the major airports, the following are open for inter-island commuter flights: **Big Island**: Hilo (General Lyman Airport), Upolu Airport, Waimea-Kohala Airport. **Kauai**: Lihue Airport, Princeville Airport. **Lanai**: Lanai City Airport. **Maui**: Hana Airport. **Molokai**: Hoolehua Airport, Kalaupapa Airport.

Hawaiian Airlines is the only local carrier with flights to the mainland. They offer extremely competitive prices, particularly for first-class, and mileage can be credited to the American Airlines Advantage program. Hawaiian Airlines also offers Air Passes for five, seven, 10 and 15 days to passengers holding return tickets on any airline.

All Thomas Cook Network locations offer airline ticket rerouting and revalidation free of charge to MasterCard holders and to travelers who have purchased their tickets through Thomas Cook.

Getting into Honolulu

There is plenty of public transportation to Honolulu, especially Waikiki. Some hotels have courtesy phones in the baggage area and will send a van for pick-up; phone immediately on arrival to save time. Fares into town are posted just outside the baggage claim area. Taxis are expensive but fast. Buses and vans are about one-third of the price but can take four times as long.

CAMPING

Camper vans, called motor homes or RVs (recreational vehicles), can be rented on all islands except Lanai. Companies are listed in the Yellow Pages under "Motor Homes – Renting and Leasing."

Hawaii is idyllic for camping, but never leave valuables in your tent. Outside the major towns there is no shortage of campsites. They are available in national, state and county parks, and some require advance reservation.

National Park Service: Prince Kuhio Federal Building, 300 Ala Moana Boulevard, Suite 6305, Box 50165, Honolulu. Tel: (808) 541–2693.

State Parks: contact the District Office of the Hawaii Department of Land and National Resources, Division of State Parks, at the following addresses. **Big Island**: PO Box 936, Hilo, HI 96720, tel: (808) 933–4200. **Kauai**: PO Box 1671, Lihue, HI 96766, tel: (808)

Barbecue time at O'ne Alii Park, Molokai

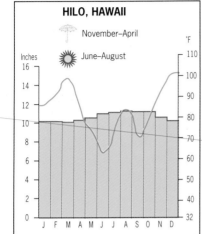

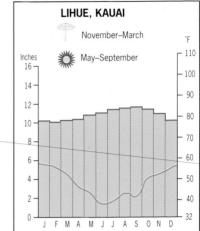

241–3444. **Maui**: PO Box 1049, Wailuku, HI 96793, tel: (808) 243–5354. **Oahu**: 1151 Punchbowl Street, Room 310, Honolulu, HI 96813, tel: (808) 587–0300.

County Parks: contact the relevant county at the following addresses. **County of Hawaii**, 25 Aupuni Street, Hilo, HI 96720, tel: (808) 961–8311. **City and County of Honolulu**, 650 South King Street, Honolulu, HI 96813, tel: (808) 523–4525. **County of Kauai**, 4444 Rice Street, Lihue, HI 96766, tel: (808) 245–8821. **County of Maui** (includes **Lanai** and **Molokai**), 1580 Kaahumanu Avenue, Wailuku, HI 96793, tel: (808) 243–7230.

CHILDREN

Throughout the area children are well catered for. Many hotels provide cots at no extra charge, while extra beds for older children are available at a nominal charge. Larger hotels offer babysitting services that are safe and reliable. The

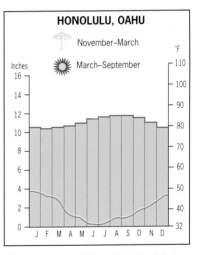

bigger resort hotels have *keiki* (activity) programs for children aged five and over. Many restaurants have children's menus or offer children's portions off the main menu. High-chairs are universally available. Children are not allowed in bars unless meals are served.

Diapers and food for infants are sold

at all supermarkets and drugstores, and in most towns from at least one convenience store 24 hours a day. Baby milk (infant formula) comes in several dairy and nondairy varieties. Prices are very reasonable.

Hawaii is generally very safe for tourists, but never leave children unattended.

Care should be taken in all coastal areas. The Pacific can be extremely dangerous, even on the most beautiful day. Take heed of all warning signs.

CLIMATE

The weather in Hawaii varies little throughout the year, with temperatures in the 70s and 80s. There are two basic seasons: April to November is marginally warmer and December to March is wetter. The sea remains at a constant 75–80°F.

CONSULATES GENERAL

For most countries the closest consulate is in California.

Australia: 1000 Bishop Street, Penthouse, Honolulu, Hawaii. Tel: (808) 524–5050.

Canada: 300 South Grand Avenue, 10th Floor, Los Angeles, CA 90071. Tel: (213) 687–7432.

Ireland: 655 Montgomery Street, San Francisco, California. Tel: (415) 392–4214.

New Zealand: 10960 Wilshire Boulevard, Suite 1530, Los Angeles, CA 90024. Tel· (?13) 477–8241.

UK: Ahmanson Center, East Building, Suite 312, 3701 Wilshire Boulevard, Los Angeles, CA 90010. Tel: (213) 385–7381.

CONVERSION TABLES

See tables opposite.

Conversion Table

FROM	TO	MULTIPLY BY
Inches	Centimeters	2.54
Feet	Meters	0.3048
Yards	Meters	0.9144
Miles	Kilometers	1.6090
Acres	Hectares	0.4047
Gallons	Liters	4.5460
Ounces	Grams	28.35
Pounds	Grams	453.6
Pounds	Kilograms	0.4536
Tons	Tonnes	1.0160

To convert back, for example from centimeters to inches, divide by the number in the the third column.

Men's Suits

UK	36	38	40	42	44	46	48
Rest of Europe	46	48	50	52	54	56	58
US	36	38	40	42	44	46	48

Dress Sizes

UK	8	10	12	14	16	18
France	36	38	40	42	44	46
Italy	38	40	42	44	46	48
Rest of Europe	34	36	38	40	42	44
US	6	8	10	12	14	16

Men's Shirts

UK	14	14.5	15	15.5	16	16.5	17
Rest of Europe	36	37	38 39/40	41		42	43
US	14	14.5	15	15.5	16	16.5	17

Men's Shoes

UK	7	7.5 0.5		9.5	10.5	11
Rest of Europe	41	42	43	44	45	46
US	8	8.5	9.5	10.5	11.5	12

Women's Shoes

UK	4.5	5	5.5	6	6.5	7
Rest of Europe	38	38	39	39	40	41
US	6	6.5	7	7.5	8	8.5

CRIME

Crime is a very real problem but should be put into perspective. It is at its worst in Honolulu but certainly not as bad as many other major cities throughout the world.

The general availability of handguns is one of the major problems, but the chances of even seeing a gun, other than on a police officer's hip, are very remote. Most shootings are in areas that tourists would rarely visit. However, it is unwise to get into a confrontation with anyone, particularly while driving. Frayed tempers have often been known to result in shootings. Also, it is unwise to pick up hitchhikers.

A very real problem is theft, from both cars and hotel rooms. Take sensible precautions and make sure valuables are not on display. Most hotel thefts are opportunist; the more difficult it is to snatch something and run, the less chance of its being stolen.

It is not advisable to walk on the beaches at night, particularly if they are away from a resort complex.

It is wise to carry travelers' checks rather than cash. All hotels and most shops and restaurants accept traveler's checks. MasterCard, Visa and American Express traveler's checks are widely recognized and provide fast service in the case of loss.

CUSTOMS REGULATIONS

Everyone entering the US must pass through US Customs. Personal allowances for visitors include one US quart of spirits or wine (32 fluid ounces), 300 cigarettes or 50 cigars, plus up to $100 worth of gifts. In practice, most of these items are far cheaper within the US than at airport duty-free shops.

The amount of currency imported or exported is not restricted, but anything over $10,000 must be declared.

US Customs are particularly concerned about drugs, animals, meat (both fresh and processed), plants and fresh fruit. Penalties are severe.

DRIVING

Drivers will need a valid licence from any country that signed the 1949 Geneva Agreement. International Driver's Permits are generally unnecessary.

Road signs use international symbols. Major roads are well surfaced and well marked. In some rural areas there are sections of unpaved road. Motorways are called freeways and other major roads are highways. Oahu has the only freeways on the islands. Lane discipline is very good, but remember that people can overtake on either side.

Theoretically, traffic is banded according to relative speed (with the fastest lane on the left), but it's not unheard of to find someone creeping along at 40mph in the fast lane. Keep your eyes open and use your mirrors frequently.

The speed limit on all highways and freeways is 55mph unless otherwise posted. In town the limit is 25 to 35mph. Speed limits are always well signposted and strictly enforced by radar on all the islands. Drink-drive laws are extremely tough, so don't even consider taking a chance.

Because of the low speed limits, driving is generally safe. In cities there is a continual problem with drivers anticipating traffic lights or trying to make it through on a yellow. Always be careful at these junctions as there is usually no yellow phase between red and green.

The Makapuu coastal road on Oahu serpentines beneath sharp lava cliffs overlooking the open sea

There are many minor junctions where there is a stop sign in only one direction, and they are often not clearly marked. Pay particular attention when driving off the main roads.

If you have to drive in Honolulu, it is a good idea to plan your journey well in advance. The one-way system can be so complicated that a missed turn-off could result in a lot of unnecessary frustration and wasted time. Honolulu has more cars per capita than any other city in the nation, which becomes quite obvious if you venture out from 6:30–8:30am or 3:30–5:30pm.

Parking

In Honolulu, Lahaina and Kailua-Kona, looking for a parking space – particularly in the town center – can be like searching for the Holy Grail. Parking restrictions are indicated by curb-side color codes. Red means no parking at any time, day or night. Yellow is strictly for commercial vehicles and is normally only in force during business hours (shown on the curb). Blue is for cars displaying a special handicapped sticker. Certain meters displaying a wheelchair symbol are also reserved exclusively for handicapped motorists. Never, ever, park in blue zones. They carry the highest parking penalty.

Street parking is generally regulated by meters, with time limits ranging from 15 minutes to four hours, and they almost all accept quarters. Feeding meters is prohibited, but common nevertheless. In business districts some meters are allocated specifically for commercial vehicles. This is clearly stated on both the meter and the curb.

Always read notices attached to meters. On major streets in cities, parking is often restricted at rush hours. During these periods you'll get a hefty parking ticket and also be towed away. If a meter is obviously broken, the usual solution is to write "Meter broken" on a paper grocery bag and place it over the meter. This usually avoids a ticket.

Fuel and maps

Hawaii is ideal for road trips, and, although gas is expensive, there is no shortage of gas stations and garage facilities. For older cars there is one grade of leaded gas. For newer models which take unleaded there is regular or super, plus a recently introduced intermediate grade of 89 octane. Use unleaded gas in rental cars. Most gas stations also sell diesel fuel.

All gas stations have good maps for sale, and most car rental companies have local maps free of charge.

The main motoring organisation in the US is the American Automobile Association (called Triple A). The AAA has reciprocal agreements with overseas motoring organizations, and both roadside assistance and free route maps are available upon presentation of your membership card.

Car rental

It is usually better to arrange for a car before arriving. Several airlines have special deals available with preferential rates if the booking is made in advance. Try to make a reservation, if possible, as certain categories of car may be in short supply during peak seasons.

Most people visiting the Islands rent a

Honolulu's forest of palm trees and street signs

car, and each time a plane lands, the rental agencies are swamped. To minimize delays, go straight to the car rental counter before picking up your baggage (security at baggage claim areas is very good). With the exception of Honolulu, all the major rental agencies have cars available within walking distance of the baggage claim area.

Local car rental firms often offer better rates than the big names. Generally, off-airport companies offer the best value, and they all provide a free shuttle service to their facility. There are dozens listed in the Yellow Pages.

Automatic transmission is standard in all rental cars. American cars are big, and a so-called midsize is huge by European standards. The smallest size available is the subcompact, which will just carry four people and a small amount of luggage. For summer travel, ask for a car with air conditioning, usually available at no extra cost.

None of the major car rental companies will rent to anyone under the age of 25. It may be possible to find a local company that will, but be prepared to pay a loaded insurance premium.

Extra collision insurance is always offered, and this can be almost 50 percent of the rental fee. Check before leaving home – you may already be covered by your own personal car insurance policy.

Breakdowns and accidents

In case of breakdown, immediately inform the car rental company and await instructions.

In case of accident:

- Set up warning signs. Flares are usually used and are available from any auto store.
- Call the police and an ambulance if required. The emergency telephone number is 911.
- Take the names and addresses of all involved, the make and licence plate number of the other vehicle, and the names and numbers of insurance policies.
- Write down names and addresses of any witnesses, together with the time and date of the accident. If possible, take photographs of the accident from several angles.
- Never, under any circumstances, admit to or sign any statement of responsibility.

ELECTRICITY

The standard supply is 110 volts at 60 cycles. Flat two-pin plugs are used universally. Converters are sold widely in the US, but it may save time to bring one from home.

EMERGENCIES

For police, fire and ambulance dial 911. The Thomas Cook Worldwide Customer Promise offers free emergency assistance at any Thomas Cook Network location to travelers who have purchased their travel tickets at a Thomas Cook location. In addition, any MasterCard cardholder may use any Thomas Cook Network location to report loss or theft of their card and obtain an emergency card replacement, as a free service under the Thomas Cook MasterCard International Alliance.

Thomas Cook travelers' check refund is a 24-hour service. Report loss or theft within 24 hours, tel: 1–800 223–7373 (toll-free).

HEALTH

Up-to-date health advice can be obtained at any Thomas Cook travel shop.

There are no mandatory vaccination requirements, and no vaccination recommendations other than to keep tetanus and polio immunization up to date.

The standard of health care is extremely high, but so are the costs. It is essential to have a good insurance policy. Many doctors and hospitals refuse to give treatment without proof of insurance.

All major hospitals have 24-hour emergency rooms. Doctors and dentists are listed at hotels or in the Yellow Pages.

Hawaii does not have many specific health problems. Food and tap water are safe, but if hiking in the backcountry do not drink from streams, as the water often carries the intestinal parasite *giardia*.

As in every other part of the world, AIDS is present.

HITCHHIKING
Hitchhiking is not recommended in Hawaii. Motorists are very wary of hitchhikers, and it can be very difficult to get lifts.

INSURANCE
Travel insurance to cover both loss of property and medical expenses is essential. Make sure that medical policies give adequate coverage, including emergency flights home. Cancellation insurance is advisable if appropriate.

LAUNDRY
All major hotels have one-day laundry and dry-cleaning services from Monday to Friday. Alternatively, many dry-cleaners offer a two- to four-hour service; check the Yellow Pages.

MAPS
General maps are available from car rental companies. More detailed town maps and walking maps are usually available free of charge at Chambers of Commerce and Visitor Bureau, which are listed in the Yellow Pages.

MEASUREMENTS
Hawaii uses the imperial system of measurement. The only difference is that UK pints, quarts and gallons are 25 per cent bigger than the US measurements of the same name (eg a US pint has 16 fluid ounces, not 20). The price of a gallon of petrol can be appreciated accordingly!

MEDIA
The closest there is to a national daily newspaper in Hawaii is the *Honolulu Advertiser*. Honolulu is also home to the *Honolulu Star Bulletin*, which is an afternoon paper owned by the giant Gannett chain. Altogether there are nine daily newspapers. Six are English language, one Chinese, one Japanese and one Korean.

In most of the bigger towns you can find both the *Wall Street Journal* and the *New York Times*, which often give a more global view of the news. *USA Today* provides a more condensed version of the news.

For local news, including weather and traffic conditions, keep the car radio tuned to one of the news stations. There are stations broadcasting in most of the main languages spoken on the Islands and catering to virtually every interest, from classical to Hawaiian, including what is known as "talk radio." These phone-in programs attract calls from the fringes of society and are usually banal at best. They can, however, be an amusing diversion and provide an insight into the American psyche.

In most parts of Hawaii it is possible to receive a Public Broadcasting Service (PBS) station. The quality of programming is better and includes the BBC News.

Virtually every hotel and motel room has a television. More often than not, it will be cable TV offering 30 or more channels. There are usually two or three PBS stations. These give good news coverage, and most of the other programmes are British productions. CNN provides excellent continuous news coverage.

MONEY MATTERS
Banking hours are from 8:30am to 3pm Monday to Thursday and often until 6pm on Fridays. There are no restrictions on the amount of money that can be either brought into or taken out of the US (see **Customs Regulations**).

A Honolulu sidewalk studded with newspaper vending machines, some of which are free sheets

State sales tax is applied to all goods and to restaurant meals.

All major credit cards are universally accepted. Travelers' checks, which must be in US dollars, are readily accepted in lieu of cash in shops, hotels and restaurants. Most banks offer foreign exchange facilities, although a dedicated *bureau de change* such as one of the Thomas Cook locations following will give a quicker and more expert service. Thomas Cook MasterCard travelers' checks free you from the hazards of carrying large amounts of cash, and in the event of loss or theft can quickly be refunded (see emergency telephone number, page 183, and emergency help location opposite).

For emergency assistance in the case of loss or theft of Thomas Cook MasterCard travelers' checks, contact: Honolulu International Airport, Honolulu (tel: 808 834–1099); Ala Moana Center, Honolulu (tel: 808 946–7888) or 830 Fort Street Mall, Honolulu (tel: 808 523–1321).

US currency is available in denominations of 1, 5, 10, 20, 50 and 100 dollar bills. There is a $2 bill, but it is rarely seen. Although all notes are exactly the same size and color, the denomination is clearly printed on each corner on both sides. If you feel unsure, stick to the lower denominations to avoid expensive mistakes. Coins come in pennies (1 cent), nickels (5 cents), dimes (10 cents), quarters (25 cents) and 50-cent pieces; 100 cents make a dollar. Quarters are handy for parking meters, telephones and newspapers.

OPENING HOURS

Most larger shops are open seven days a week, typically from 10am to 6pm and to noon on Sundays. Smaller shops and more specialized businesses close on Sundays. Most offices, including government offices, open Monday to Friday 8:30am to 5pm. Museums and art galleries vary dramatically. Recent budget deficits have resulted in severely curtailed opening hours at many state museums, and it is always wise to check before a visit.

ORGANIZED TOURS

The majority of people visiting Hawaii rent cars, which is undoubtedly the best way to see the state. If time is limited, a tour may be the best solution. Particularly in Honolulu, tours can save parking headaches and ensure that nothing major is missed.

There are both ordinary and specialized tours available in profusion. If time is limited, an ordinary tour may fit the bill, but it will be fairly superficial and with a large busload of fellow tourists. Specialized tours cater for specific interests and are usually with smaller groups of people. Dozens of tour operators serve Hawaii; hotels can usually advise on what is available. Also look in the weekly free tourist publications such as *Spotlight Hawaii* or *This Week* for details of current offerings.

NATIONAL HOLIDAYS

New Year's Day (1 January)
Martin Luther King Day (3rd Monday in January)
Lincoln's Birthday (12 February)
Washington's Birthday (3rd Monday in February)
Memorial Day (last Monday in May)
Independence Day (4 July)
Labor Day (1st Monday in September)
Columbus Day (2nd Monday in October)
Veterans Day (11 November)
Thanksgiving (4th Thursday in November)
Christmas (25 December).

Peak periods for travel, hotels and campsites are Memorial Day, Independence Day and Labor Day. Air travel peaks at Thanksgiving and Christmas. Government offices, including post offices, are closed for most national holidays, but few places observe them all. Shops remain open on all but Thanksgiving and Christmas.

PHARMACIES

Most pharmacies are open from at least 9am to 6pm, and many have longer hours. Drugstores, despite the name, are like mini-supermarkets and have a wide range of products on sale, including wine and spirits, hardware and snacks, as well as a pharmacy counter for dispensing prescriptions; they are usually open until

9pm. The Yellow Pages gives a complete list of pharmacies.

Many nonprescription drugs can be obtained from ordinary supermarkets.

PLACES OF WORSHIP

Virtually every religion known to man has a presence in the Islands. Newspapers generally list times of services for the main denominations. A complete list, including mosques and Buddhist temples, can be found under "Churches" in the Yellow Pages. Synagogues have their own listing.

POLICE

Every incorporated city in Hawaii has its own police force with normal police responsibilities, including traffic control. In case of any emergency, the telephone number to call throughout Hawaii is 911.

POST OFFICES

Post offices are generally open Monday to Friday from 8 or 8:30am to 4 or 4:30pm and 10am–noon on Saturdays. They are always closed on Sundays. Post boxes (mail boxes) are blue with "US Mail" written on them in white. Postage rates may change during your visit, so always check. Stamps from vending machines in hotels and shops cost more than from a post office. An airmail letter or postcard takes at least one week to travel from Hawaii to Europe (surface mail has been known to take three months!).

Parcels must be properly packaged and, if being sent by registered mail,

nonremovable, non-shiny tape must be used. Appropriate containers are sold at post offices. A Customs declaration form must accompany any parcel being mailed abroad.

Poste restante is known as "General Delivery." Letters can be addressed to any post office and must include the zip code. Mail is held for only 30 days, after which it is returned to the sender, whose name and address must be on the outside of the envelope. When collecting General Delivery mail, you need some form of identification.

Telegrams are sent from Western Union offices, not from post offices. If you have a credit card, you can dictate a telegram over the telephone and charge it. Western Union offices are listed in the Yellow Pages.

PUBLIC TRANSPORTATION

See page 20.

SENIOR CITIZENS

Most hotels, motels, restaurants and museums have preferential rates for senior citizens. Usually they want to see some form of identification, but often just looking old enough is sufficient – which can be very demoralizing!

SMOKING

Throughout the USA smoking has declined so dramatically that smokers are generally looked upon as social pariahs. In Hawaii, the tobacco habit is rapidly becoming the exception rather than the rule, although the strong presence of

Japanese tourists ensures its survival. Smoking is not allowed on public transportation or in any public building. Many workplaces have banned it too.

Most hotels offer nonsmoking rooms, and car rental companies offer smoke-free cars. Restaurants still have small smoking sections, but they are small indeed.

TELEPHONES

In Hawaii you are never far from a phone, and most of them work. Apart from telephone kiosks (booths) in the street, there are payphones in most bars, restaurants and hotel lobbies.

All public telephones accept nickels, dimes and quarters (5, 10 and 25-cent coins) with 25 cents being the minimum charge. In airports there are often telephones that allow the call to be charged to a credit card.

Hotels usually charge a high premium for calls from the room. Conversely, some hotels allow local calls at no cost. Always check the rates.

Reverse-charge calls, called collect calls, can be made from any telephone through the operator. Dial 0 for the local operator or 00 for a long-distance operator.

All numbers with an 800 or 1–800 prefix are toll-free. At a public telephone insert a dime first, which will be returned when you replace the handset.

For international calls dial 011, the country code and then the number. The cheapest time for overseas calls is 11pm–7am. International codes are: Australia 61; Ireland 353; New Zealand 64; UK 44. Canada has no country code from the US.

Directory inquiries: local, dial 411; long-distance, dial the relevant area code, then 555–1212; toll-free inquiries, dial (800) 555–1212.

TIME

Hawaii is on Hawaii Standard Time, which is 10 hours behind GMT. Daylight saving time is not in effect in Hawaii, so the clocks don't change in spring and autumn.

TIPPING

Tips are a way of life, and everyone in the service industry expects them. They are very rarely included in the bill, except occasionally in restaurants for large parties. Always check. The amount is, of course, always at the discretion of the customer, but this is a general guide:
15 percent: restaurants, bars, taxis, room service
10 percent: hairdresser
$2: room maid (per day)
$1: cloakroom attendant, parking valet, tour guide or driver (per day), hotel and airport porters (per bag)
50 cents: shoeshine, toilet attendant.

TOILETS

Public toilets, called restrooms, are not always easy to find, but when you do they are almost always clean and free. In Honolulu they can be found in large department stores, bars and restaurants, and all gas stations.

TOURIST OFFICES

The Hawaii Visitors Bureaux can provide maps, brochures and referrals to local Chambers of Commerce for more specific information. Contact them at:
Big Island: 250 Keawe Street, Hilo, HI 96720, tel: (808) 961–5797; 75–5719 West Ali'i Drive, Kailua-Kona, HI 96740, tel: (808) 329–7787.
Kauai: Lihune Plaza Building, 3016 Umi Street, Lihue, HI 96766, tel: (808) 245–3971.
Maui: 1727 Wili Pa Loop, Wailuku,

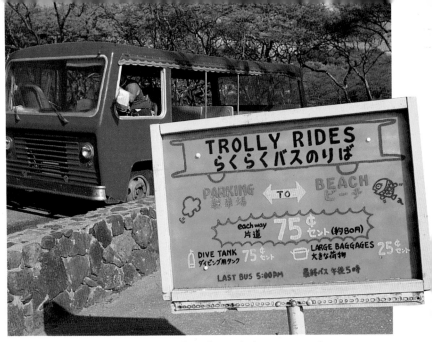

Take a trip to Hanauma Bay and explore an extinct submerged volcano, now a marine preserve

HI 96793, tel: (808) 244–3530.
Oahu: Waikiki Business Plaza, 2270 Kalakaua Avenue, Suite 801, Honolulu, HI 96815, tel: (808) 923–1811.

TRAVELERS WITH DISABILITIES

The US is more responsive to the needs of disabled people than many countries. Airports have good facilities, including special lifts, toilets and wheelchairs.

Most hotels, public buildings and museums now have wheelchair access and toilet facilities, but check that your destination has adequate facilities.

Handicapped parking areas, marked with a wheelchair symbol, are widely available, and hefty fines are levied for illegal use of these spaces.

Throughout Hawaii people are sympathetic to the problems of the disabled and generally very helpful. The Commission on Persons with Disabilities publishes an accessibility guide to hotels, shopping centers, beaches and other attractions. It also lists addresses and telephone numbers of support services for disabled visitors. For information contact: 5 Waterfront Plaza, Suite 210, 500 Ala Moana Boulevard, Honolulu, HI 96813, tel: (808) 586–8121.

WHAT TO TAKE

Most people find that they take too much to Hawaii. At sea level the temperature is always comfortable and you will rarely need more than lightweight clothing. Formal dress is never required, even in the poshest restaurants. Remember to take strong sun protection and anything to keep off the rain. If you do forget something, you can always buy it in Hawaii (often for less than at home). For sports enthusiasts, equipment can be rented wherever the activity takes place.

ACKNOWLEDGMENTS

The Automobile Association wishes to thank the following photographers, libraries and organizations for their assistance in the preparation of this book.
ALOHA FESTIVALS 155 (Ric Noyle); ALA MOANA CENTER 148, 164; BISHOP MUSEUM 35a (David Franzen), 35b; THE RONALD GRANT ARCHIVE 71a, 71b; HAWAII OPERA THEATER 151; HAWAII STATE ARCHIVES 16b, 17; HAWAII VISITORS BUREAU 162 (B Romerhaus); HAWAII VOLCANOES NATIONAL PARK 9 (J D Griggs), 99b; HONOLULU SYMPHONY SOCIETY 150; THE KOBAL COLLECTION 70a (Paramount), 70b (Paramount); LAKE COUNTY (IL) MUSEUM, CURT TEICH ARCHIVES 169a; THE MANSELL COLLECTION LTD 10; NATIONAL MARITIME MUSEUM 100, 101a, 101b; SPECTRUM COLOUR LIBRARY 4, 27, 163a; WAIKIKI AQUARIUM 51 (Tom Kelly); ZEFA PICTURES LTD 29, 127, 140b, 142b, 181
The remaining photographs were taken by Robert Holmes.

The author would like to thank the following people and institutions for additional help: Gail Chew, the Hawaii Visitors Bureau; Julia Gadjek; Noelani Whittington; Maurice and Marjorie Holmes; and his wife Bobbie and daughters Emma and Hannah.

CONTRIBUTORS

Series adviser: Melissa Shales   **Designer:** Design 23   **Copy editor:** Janet Tabinski
Verifier: Joanna Whitaker   **Indexer:** Marie Lorimer